114498

S0-CBQ-974

R$_x$: THE CHRISTIAN LOVE TREATMENT

DR. ALPHONSE CALABRESE
and WILLIAM PROCTOR

G.K.HALL &CO.

 Boston, Massachusetts

1977

Library of Congress Cataloging in Publication Data

Calabrese, Alphonse.
   R$_x$, the Christian love treatment.

"Published in large print."
   1. Christianity—Psychology. 2. Psychoanalysis and
religion. 3. Christian life—1960- 4. Calabrese,
Alphonse. 5. Large type books. I. Proctor, William,
joint author. II. Title.
[BR110.C33 1977] 201'.9 77-12649
ISBN 0-8161-6524-6

Copyright © 1976 by Alphonse Calabrese and William
Proctor

All Rights Reserved

Published in Large Print by arrangement with
Doubleday & Company, Inc.

Set in Compugraphic 18 pt English Times

Biblical excerpts from *The Jerusalem Bible,* copyright
© 1966 by Darton, Longman & Todd, Ltd. and
Doubleday & Company, Inc. Used by permission of
the publishers.

201.9
C125r

L.I.F.E. College Library
1100 Glendale Blvd.
Los Angeles, Calif. 90026

R$_x$: THE CHRISTIAN LOVE TREATMENT

028451

Preface

After counseling thousands of men and women with every variety of emotional problem during the past two decades, I've become quite reluctant to give pat answers or make sweeping generalizations about mental and spiritual health. In this book, I have mentioned some of the common threads that distinguish anxieties, depressions, and other psychological disturbances. But because unique backgrounds and personal experiences are so decisive in causing mental difficulties, I've relied mostly on descriptions of actual patients, whose identities are either disguised or presented as composites to protect confidential disclosures. These concrete illustrations demonstrate better than any abstract discourse how you and your loved ones can improve your own emotional and spiritual well-being.

Were I to include the names of all the people whom God has sent to cross my path in my moving toward eternity who are responsible for the point at which I now find myself, and to whom I am forever indebted, it would read like the New York City Telephone Directory. I owe everything, including salvation, to these people whom God has used for this purpose.

First of all, I thank my parents for their living example of the truth that "it is better to give than to receive." To my father I owe the fact that he lived and taught me almost nonverbally that we must never compromise with truth and that we must "say it like it is," no matter what the consequences. My mother taught me a depth of love and generosity which extended beyond our immediate family to the community. She loved people dearly. She also instilled in a me a hunger for books and learning.

I owe to many priests, sisters, brothers, ministers, holy people (some unsophisticated, some learned) the joy of discovering God and worshiping him.

I would like to thank Father Cosmos Shaughnessey, C.P., a beautiful person, a Passionist monk, who in my early youth led me with such love and patience "to see first the Kingdom of God." He has been with the Lord now for a few years, but he lives in the lives of those of us he has brought to the Lord.

I am grateful to my present pastor, Father Henry Palmer, for the fact that in the three years of my desert experience he was always a silent "light on the hill" for me, never judging, and always sharing with no trace of shame for his own weaknesses. He has truly been one of the most significant men in my later adult life.

I am indebted to many lay people — Peg Matuozzi, a dear friend and charismatic Christian who came to me for healing. We were healed together — she by her prayers, humor, patience, and the homily which her whole life preaches. She helped bring me back to "what my heart and soul sought for." To Roberta Cochrane, who also by her prayers was a powerhouse that helped me back to God; to Vinnie Barbato, the person who tapped me on the shoulder at a meeting and said to me, an absolute stranger, "Something in me is moving me to tell you my story." To my children (all eight of them) for the patience they exhibited as they lost part of their father in my training and the long arduous clinical work. To my wife, Florence, who has been a support, never a hindrance, and an anchorage "cautioning here, following there, but always with love."

I am grateful to Billy Graham, whom the Lord chose to be the precipitating factor that would change my whole life on that blessed night when I accepted the Lord; also to Rev. Stephen Olford of Calvary Baptist Church, whose radio programs were so helpful to me after my conversion. I must also mention Rev. David H. C. Reed of Madison Avenue Presbyterian Church, whose radio homilies were tremendously influential.

Last but not least, I must mention my

cousin and brother and confrere Rudy Calabrese, who was a support and an example in our work.

For all these people I am profoundly thankful. My life is so much richer and more joyous for their presence, and to a small degree this book is my way of saying "thank you."

Contents

Part One:
FROM FREUD
TO JESUS

Chapter One

A Funny Thing Happened
on the Way to the Crusade

Billy Graham had always seemed like a professional religious huckster to me. I had seen him a couple of times on television, and I enjoyed ridiculing him, so my wife, Florence, thought it was somewhat strange that I wanted to drive into Manhattan one Sunday to one of his crusades in Madison Square Garden.

"I've decided to do some research for an article on conversion and mob psychology," I explained to her as we sat in our Long Island living room. "I've made up a questionnaire I want to hand out to some of those kooks who say they've made 'decisions for Christ.' "

Florence shook her head. "You're

working six days a week already. Now it's seven with this project. Well, I'm not going to give my husband up completely. If you're going, the kids and I will go with you."

Reluctantly, I agreed. We have eight kids, and I could already imagine the hassle of keeping track of them in the crowd at the Garden. But Florence was right about one thing: I *had* been spending too much time at work. During the fifteen years that I had been working as an orthodox Freudian psychoanalyst, my business had boomed. In a Park Avenue office on Manhattan's posh Upper East Side, I had developed an extremely lucrative practice among television, film, and stage celebrities. At another office I had recently opened up on Long Island, a number of wealthy businessmen and their families were regular clients. The money was rolling in, and I had to turn many people away.

Still, for some reason — perhaps a desire to enhance my scholarly credentials — I wanted to devote part of my leisure time to some research. As we drove down the Long Island Expressway, I began to think I was making a mistake. Seven of our eight kids were in the station wagon with us, a torrential rain had slowed our progress to a crawl.

"The kids are going to get pneumonia in this weather!" Florence complained. "Why don't we just turn back?"

"No!" I retorted. "You wanted to come along, so you'll just have to put up with the weather — as well as with Graham's preaching."

I'll have to admit that I had considered turning back, and if my wife hadn't been in the car with me, I probably would have. But I felt I had to be unwavering — or stubborn, as the case might be — to show her she couldn't change my mind about something as important as a scientific research project. When we arrived at the Garden, we couldn't find a parking place at first. We drove around and around Manhattan's West Side, until I finally found a space about ten blocks from the auditorium.

The kids were fretting, trying to keep dry as we ran up the street toward the

Garden. When we finally reached the entrance, an attendant dealt the final blow to our ill-starred outing: "Sorry. No more seats. You'll have to try another night."

"I told you we should have turned back," Florence reminded me. "You should have known something like this would happen."

I knew I was beaten, so I shrugged and said, "Well, you're right. That's that. Let's find a restaurant, get a hamburger or something and head back home."

But as we walked along the side of the huge Garden building, a funny thing happened. A man stuck his head out of one of the side exits and called us over. "You want some seats for the crusade?"

"Sure," I replied. "But there are nine of us."

I started to walk away, but he stopped me: "That's exactly how many seats I've got — nine, up on the front row."

Amazed at our luck, we immediately followed him inside and few minutes later found ourselves inthe cavernous Felt Forum, looking up at the huge choir which formed a background for Billy

Graham and other dignitaries who were sitting on the speaker's platform. The spectacle had already started, and I began to take mental notes of what was going on around me so that I could record my impressions later when I wrote my scholarly paper. The Reverend Stephen Olford, the English preacher who has his own syndicated television program, had just finished praying, and the choir under the direction of Cliff Barrows, began to belt out an old-time Gospel hymn. About one hundred deafmutes sat in one section of the choir and translated the words of the hymn through sign language. Always the detached analyst, I sat unmoved.

Then Graham himself got up to preach. His staccato speech and forceful gestures somehow seemed more impressive in person than they ever had on television. His topic was on young people, and though I can't remember the exact words, his message went something like this: "Students are searching for something today, but they're not finding it . . . narcotics addiction is up . . . they want something more than the material things that are being offered them . . . Jesus said, who among you would give your brother a stone when he asks for bread, or a serpent when he asks for fish? . . . these young people, and their elders as well, need Jesus Christ.''

Graham then invited those who were interested in making a commitment to Christ to come forward. The whole show had failed to affect me one bit. I leaned over to Florence and whispered, "Here come the crazies now!" The choir sang "Just as I Am," and hundreds of businessmen, hippies, housewives, representatives of every race — even several Indians wearing turbans — moved out of their seats and down the aisles. I was especially amazed at the number of young people. They were exuding a kind of joy that I couldn't quite fathom.

Then the evangelist seemed ready to end the meeting. Most of the movement forward had ended, and the choir had stopped singing. Graham raised his hands in the air and said, "You know, one time long ago, five minutes meant the difference in my own salvation. I was listening to an evangelist, and he extended his call. I came forward myself during that extra five minutes. Perhaps there are some here tonight who are on the verge of committing themselves to Jesus. I'm going to ask the choir to sing softly once more. If you feel the Spirit of God moving you, won't you join us?"

As he spoke and the choir began to move through another verse of "Just as I am, without one plea . . ." a warm feeling began to steal over me. I distrusted it. *Be careful!* a voice inside me seemed to say. *It's mob psychology! It's part of the whole game here, part of the way this guy is manipulating everybody.* I clutched my questionnaires and steeled myself against these irrational forces that I, as a trained student of the human mind, believed were threatening my good sense and sound judgment.

I might have made it through that evening too, except for one small, unexpected factor — my youngest child, eight-year-old Jimmy. As the last seconds of the invitation ticked away, he hooked his thin little arm through mine and asked,

9

"Daddy, why don't we give our hearts to Jesus?"

Suddenly, it all came together. Years of nominal Roman Catholicism, boring religious training, heckling street corner evangelists — yes, it all came together for me at that moment. Jimmy's question was like the last grain of precipitate that saturates a solution and causes a shower of crystals to form before your eyes.

"Okay, let's go," I said.

My seven children and my wife followed me up to the front, and, with tears welling up in our eyes, we declared with our hearts as well as our lips, "I accept Jesus Christ as my Lord and Savior."

It was tough to grow up as the only Italian kid in a heavily Irish neighborhood in Brooklyn in the 1920s. The fact that my family was Roman Catholic helped a little, but I was still shunned by many of the other children as "that guinea." My father had emigrated from Naples, Italy, in 1906 and found a job in Brooklyn as an apprentice cobbler. By the time I was born in 1923, he had his own store. Even though he didn't make a great deal of money and sometimes had to make a sale one day to pay the light bill and buy the groceries the next, we managed fairly well. When he had saved enough money, he sent for the rest of his family, who still lived in Naples — six brothers, one sister, and his mother.

My mother, whose parents also came from Italy, made sure I went to Mass and confession once a week, but I became more a cultural than committed Roman Catholic. She died at age thirty-eight, when I was only twelve years old. That was one of the great tragedies of my life. My father immediately took over the full responsibility of rearing me and my four sisters.

As I got older, I decided I would like to be a priest because, for a lone Italian in a rather hostile Irish neighborhood, that was one of the best careers for upward social mobility. When I announced I was going to be a priest, doors started swinging open as teachers and neighbors started paying more attention to me. The only disapproval I got was from my father. He was concerned about who was going to carry on the family name because I was his only son. But it wasn't his objections that deterred me. I entered seminary and after a couple of years learned through experience that I couldn't take the celibate life. So I dropped out and started working toward a bachelor's degree in sociology at St. John's University.

This time, it was my father's turn to be disappointed. He had gotten used to the idea of having a son who would be a priest and recognized that my cousins would be able to carry on the family name. Besides, he had found there were many fringe benefits for an Italian father whose son was going to be ordained. When he had first moved to the Green Point section of Brooklyn, people smashed his windows and harassed him because he was an Italian. But now, as the father of a prospective priest, he had become a big shot in the Catholic War Veterans and the Knights of Columbus. I'm not claiming all the credit, but my choice of profession had not hurt his social status.

After dropping out of seminary, I found

I was still interested in counseling people, so after a couple of false starts as a teacher and a law student, I ended up at Catholic University in Washington, D.C., and became a psychiatric social worker. One thing led to another, and at the suggestion of some psychiatrists who had been impressed with me as a social worker, I applied for an won a twenty-five-thousand-dollar fellowship at the Postgraduate Center for Mental Health in New York City. That was a tremendous turning point in my life because I was able to become a certified psychoanalyst and pick up a Ph.D. through a separate study program. Without this financial help, I would never have been able to complete the courses at the center and the required four-year program of undergoing psychoanalysis. I had all eight kids when I entered the center, and my wife was facing some health problems at the time. I would have been unable to scrape up the money by myself.

Somewhere in this odyssey from poor Italian kid from Brooklyn to Manhattan psychoanalyst, I began to shed the cultural

Roman Catholicism that had been so much a part of my family's life. I still went to Mass occasionally for the sake of my children, but the Church and the Christian faith seemed irrelevant to me. Sigmund Freud had taken the place of Jesus in my life. I was exposed to the giants in the field of psychoanalysis, many of whom had been students of Freud himself. They convinced me that all emotional problems could be solved if you probed far enough into the subconscious personality. I accepted a completely deterministic philosophy of life which assumed that a person's background and early family influences forced him to act in certain predetermined ways. Sexual development, I decided, was behind many if not all emotional ills. Repression of sexual impulses and feelings led to unhealthy personality development.

These ideas came more and more into conflict with my traditional Christian upbringing, and the teachings of Freud consistently triumphed over those of Jesus. Premarital or extramarital intercourse might be all right, I concluded, if the departure from traditional morality helped the individual function better sexually. Self-fulfillment took precedence over responsibility and faithfulness to others. More and more, I accepted a mythological approach to Christianity: The story of Noah and the Ark was not historically true. Instead, it just covered up some higher insight. If we could strip away the fictional trappings of the biblical account, we might find the theological essence. I also decided Jesus probably hadn't really arisen from the dead. My list of biblical items to be "demythologized" went on until little was left of the Scriptures.

Sometimes my education in Freudian faith was a little painful, but I learned fairly quickly. During one professional seminar, a student announced that he had been counseling a young woman who couldn't relate meaningfully to men. He explained that she was twenty-five years old and a virgin, and the professor in charge of the session asked, "Why don't you encourage her to have an affair?"

Somewhat disconcerted, the student

responded, "Where will she find a man?"

"Is she attractive?" the professor asked with a slight smile.

"Yes, but . . ."

"Then tell her to go anywhere and find one. Use your imagination. It's a shame that this girl has reached the age of twenty-five and has never had intercourse."

Still somewhat naive in the ways of proper psychotherapeutic amorality, I piped up with what I thought was a reasonably pertinent point: "Is it really a shame that she hasn't had intercourse? Or is it a shame that she's reached the age of twenty-five and has never had a man tell her that he loves her?"

I was completely unprepared for the reaction that followed. Several students laughed at me, pooh-poohed my comments, or engaged in outright ridicule: "Oh, come on, Al, do you think this is still the Middle Ages? Do you want to make this poor girl feel guilty?"

Crushed, I retreated into an embarrassed silence. I had only been trying to raise a point for discussion, not challenge

16

the very foundations of Freudian psychoanalysis. The student therapist followed the professor's advice and told the young woman to find herself a bedmate. She complied and got a venereal disease. That struck me as a worse result than if she had remained a virgin, but the professor shrugged off the problem. "That's an infection that can be treated medically," he told the student. "It's your job to keep working with her and be sure she isn't overcome by guilt feelings."

I never felt quite comfortable with this approach to psychotherapy, perhaps because my cultural Catholicism kept whispering, *something is very seriously wrong here!* Although I never accepted an amoral approach to sex in my own life, I became quite bold in encouraging adultery and premarital sex in some of my counseling sessions.

One young man named Frank came to me after I had set up a private practice on Park Avenue. "I have some real problems in my sexual relationship with my wife," he said. "She can't stand love-making, and I really get frustrated. But I find when she's finally ready, I sometimes can't respond. I have these fantasies about women I meet, especially this one secretary in my office." He sighed morosely. "I feel like a real loser."

"Have you ever considered doing something about your fantasies?" I asked, with my usual pre-Christian lack of moral sensitivity.

"What do you mean?"

"I mean if you started having more regular sexual relations, you might find your own inability to perform would disappear."

"Oh, I couldn't sleep with someone who wasn't my wife."

"Why not?"

"It's wrong, isn't it? I mean, I was always taught adultery was wrong."

"Who taught you that?"

"My parents, my church leaders. I was brought up in a Christian background."

"You have to forget these feelings you have about superficial rights and wrongs and get to the root of your problem," I replied.

We then began to explore his early

childhood experiences, especially his relationship with his mother. She had been an unloving woman and he had felt unwanted. She has stressed that sex was dirty and abstaining from intimate contact was a virtue. Subconsciously, Frank had married a woman who also represented this false ideal. Through his marriage relationship he was trying to heal the hurt he had felt from his mother, but once again, he found himself failing miserably.

As we talked, I could see a natural resentment welling up in him toward his mother and his wife. But I refrained from reminding him that he had a responsibility for anyone besides himself. In Freudian therapy, a sense of responsibility for others is by no means a cardinal virtue, and may be a decided drawback. I never actually told Frank to find another woman and have an affair, but I imagine my approach in our discussions gave him the impression that I approved. After several sessions, he came in and said, "Well, I did it!"

"Did what?" I asked.

"I asked that secretary in my office out

and slept with her."

"Umm," I replied noncommittally. "And how do you feel now?"

"Pretty good, actually," he said. "We hit it off all right. I'm going to see her again tonight."

"Well, I'm gratified to see you're working out your sexual problems," I told him. "For the first time, you feel your power and attractiveness as a man. And you're breaking out of this pattern of seeing women as basically depriving. You see now how distorted your self-image was before, don't you?"

He said he did, and I suppose I should have felt satisfied. But I felt a twinge of uncertainty inside, as though there might have been something inherently wrong with what Frank had done. I expressed my reservations to a professor, but he said, "What that fellow does had nothing to do with you so long as it helps him. You have to be nonjudgmental about this. Your job is not to judge the morals of another person. You have to analyze, that's all."

I even brought the subject up with a priest I knew. "There are certain consequences for this guy's family if he starts playing around," I said.

"That's not your job to worry about that," the priest reassured me.

Having overcome my reservations through this reinforcement from other professional counselors, I became completely nondirective and relativistic in my relationships with my patients. If a young woman was involved in promiscuous sexual relationships with several men, I would never question whether the promiscuity itself was wrong. The issue, in my mind, was only what the promiscuity indicated about the woman's inability to form meaningful human relationships.

I developed something of a reputation among stars in the communications media, on the Broadway stage and in films after my Park Avenue practice had become established. One popular young actress — Suzy — came to me for help because she said she was depressed.

"I've just had this affair . . . with my casting director," she explained. "I've already been divorced once, and here I am getting involved again, and it's not working out. What's wrong with me, that's what I want to know? I've achieved a lot, have a lot of money, but life just doesn't seem to mean anything. I don't understand myself.''

As we talked, I learned that she had been involved sexually with quite a few men in the past few years. Her former husband and the casting director were only the most recent of a long string of lovers. My approach to therapy, which is employed by most psychoanalysts, was to get her to open up about her early family background so that I could determine what traumas in her childhood were influencing her adult behavior. Suzy's main problem was that her depression resulted from repressed anger and rage toward her mother. Her mother had withheld love from her and manipulated and exploited to get Suzy to do things as a child. In moving from one male lover to another, Suzy was reaching out symbolically to her mother for love and the healing that such love would bring. But these men, like her mother, exploited her. They used her sexually, just as her mother had used her emotionally.

After isolating this problem, I told Suzy that she should feel free to vent her anger toward her mother, get it out into the open and resolve it. Then she could set her relationship with her mother straight and move on to more meaningful relations with other people. Few Christian therapists would have disagreed with my technique up to this point, but the next step I took would have presented them with some difficulties. Suzy got involved in an extramarital affair with still another man while I was counseling her, but I assumed a noncommittal moral attitude toward what she was doing. My main concern was whether this new sexual relationship was more meaningful than the previous ones. I really didn't care whether or not her actions were acceptable or unacceptable to theologians, moralists, or God Himself, for that matter.

But after her new love affair had been going on for a few weeks, Suzy hit me with the one question I couldn't handle. "Dr. Calabrese," she said, "you know I'm getting along much better with this new fellow than I did with the others. I mean, we talk about things we're interested in — our careers and so forth. I do things for him and he does things for me. We make sacrifices for each other. It's not just a bedroom scene. But there's one thing that keeps bothering me. What's it all about?''

''What do you mean?'' I asked, somewhat disconcerted.

''I mean, what's it all about — this relationship, my career, all of it? Life? What's life all about?''

''The meaning of life, you mean?'' I said, clearing my throat and stuttering slightly.

''Yes.''

It was a devastating question to put to me or to most psychoanalysts, for that matter. Although I had no idea about the meaning of life, I knew I had to come up with something, so I mumbled a few words: ''I'm me, and you're you, and there are many paths to meaning and self-actualization but as we experience this great adventure called life, we must seek that stable center of personality . . .'' But

I didn't know what I was talking about. Suzy nodded, and may even have thought I was saying something profound. But I suspect she quickly realized she wouldn't receive any spiritual revelations from my direction.

Nor was Suzy the first patient who had confronted me with this question about the meaning of life. She was only the latest in a long line of people whom I could help up to a point with their emotional hang-ups, but not beyond that point. I couldn't lead them toward any answers about man's position in the universe because I didn't know what the answers were myself.

"It's not your job to get into those issues," other psychotherapists told me. "Stick to helping these people with their emotional problems, and let the priests and ministers worry about the souls — provided there is any such thing as a soul."

But such arguments didn't satisfy me. I sensed that emotional problems and problems with the spirit or soul or whatever you wanted to call it were connected. Freudians have made a great contribution in categorizing different parts of man's mind for purposes of analysis; but in the last analysis, man is a whole being. If a woman like Suzy was worried about the meaning of life, that concern was eventually going to aggravate her depressions and affect her ability to relate to others. I was annoyed that I couldn't give people like her an answer to their spiritual problems, but I simply lacked the resources.

My lack of spiritual roots soon showed up in my children. They had been brought up on the same Roman Catholic religion that I had been taught as a child, but unlike my own father and mother, I encouraged them to say exactly what they thought.

The oldest, Chuck, announced one day, "I don't believe in God."

Then Teresa, who was a year younger, said, "I don't know if God exists."

One by one they began to refuse to go to Mass. They were falling down like spiritual dominoes. What had I done wrong? When I looked at my own spiritual development, I could see that they were taking essentially the same path that I had chosen. Mass and other religious observances had become less meaningful to me. I had been brought up to believe that if you ate fish on Fridays and followed certain other practices, you'd go to heaven. But this legalism crumbled in the 1960s with the reforms instituted by Pope John at Vatican II. Many of the old comfortable rituals had become optional. I no longer had anything external, any outward signs or practices to hang my hat on. And there was certainly nothing inside me, no firm faith, to make my religion meaningful.

Psychoanalysis had filled part of the void that Catholicism had once occupied, but I needed something more. I decided to spend some time with professors back at the analytic institute to see if they could give me the answers, the ultimate meaning in life, that I was searching for.

One of them, a brilliant psychiatrist and cancer specialist whom I had always respected, said, "Life is absurd." But shortly after I began to meet with him, he was struck by cancer himself. All the signs of terminal illness were there — rectal blockage, surgical procedures, pain. Yet this man, who had told me life was absurd, refused to accept death and desperately tried to hold onto the absurdity. One week before his death he asked me to go to his office and check to see if one of his case files had been brought up to date because he expected to be back at work shortly. He denied what any observer could see was happening to him. He weighed practically nothing and could hardly sit up in bed. Shortly afterward, he went into a coma and passed away.

Another renowned psychoanalyst assured me that "life is a Charlie Chaplin comedy. Make the most of it, Al!" I knew I couldn't buy that, even as the words came out of his mouth, because there had been too much tragedy in my life. I had seen my little three-year-old sister crushed under the wheels of a truck on the streets of Brooklyn. My own sorrow was compounded by the agony that I saw this accident cause my parents, who suffered emotional wounds that never healed. Only five years after my sister's death, my mother began to die slowly, painfully, of cancer, even though she was still a young woman in her late thirties. After she died, the nation was in the depths of the Great Depression, and my father had to act as a mother and father to us, as eked out a living. I knew of the horrors of the Nazi concentration camps. I had seen the miracle of one of my daughters being born because I had to act as obstetrician on the Southern State Parkway. There was nothing funny about any of these experiences. Life for me had had its light moments, but I could never characterize it as a "Charlie Chaplin comedy."

I decided to give the psychoanalytic gurus one more chance by taking a course on the meaning of life. The title of the course was "The Meaning of Meaning," the professor said in his first lecture that the basic problem in life centers on the answer to the profound question, "What is, 'what is'?" By the end of the course, I was saying, "So what?" My search for meaning seemed fated to end in a morass of boredom and discontent.

When I boarded the Long Island Rail Road train on Monday mornings, I was struck with how much it resembled the depressed ward of a hospital. Many commuters saw their jobs as only a means to pay for the weekends. Boredom, anger, and depression were etched on their faces, and I knew they were mirror images of myself. People sometimes ask me, "How could you have been bored with your celebrity practice on Park Avenue? Millions of people buy these screen magazines to find out only half the things you heard from film and television stars in your office!"

It wasn't that my clients weren't interesting. The problem was with me. I was bored because I had been doing the same thing for fifteen years and didn't know where my work was taking me. I could see that other people, as well as myself, had problems that went deeper than psychoanalysis could probe, and I didn't know how to find the answers.

The Long Island Rail Road also looks like a hospital ward during the trip home in the evenings, but this time all the patients appear to be anesthetized. Liquor is the prime drug, and drinking had become a problem for me, too, by the mid-1960s. By 2:00 P.M. every day I was feeling good with two stiff martinis under my belt for lunch. I had another martini in the afternoon during my first break between patients, and was already looking forward to another at the four o'clock coffee break. Then I had another martini before dinner, and two more during dinner, as well as a glass of wine. I usually finished the day off with a cognac.

I never thought I got drunk, but my wife, Florence, told me later, "I knew when you had been drinking, Al. I could tell. You were a little silly and your speech was a little slurred, but you didn't realize it."

I know now that I was heading toward alcoholism. One election day, I remember going into a panic because I couldn't find any liquor around the office, and all the stores were closed. My drinking was part of a long-standing tradition among the psychotherapists I knew. Alcoholism was a big problem with some of my professors. If someone had established an Alcoholics

31

Anonymous for professional therapists, there would have been plenty of candidates among New York City head-shrinkers.

Morally and spiritually, I had hit rock bottom. Then I learned that an individual was abusing and theatening to ruin the life of a member of my family whom I loved very much. Rage welled up in me as I tried to reason with the man but found him to be insensitive and uninterested in listening. At that point, I actually began to contemplate murder.

With this thought gnawing at my insides, I went to an Italian restaurant with my wife and was beginning to calm down a little when a big, burly man walked up to me and asked, "Are you Dr. Alphonse Calabrese?"

I hesitated for a moment and then answered, "Yes."

"Mr. A. [a well-known underworld figure I had read about in the newspapers] would like to talk to you," the man said and pointed toward a small group of men who were looking in my direction.

"I don't know any Mr. A.," I replied, hoping the guy would leave me alone. The last thing I needed now was to get mixed up with organized crime.

The bodyguard — at least I think that's what his job was — walked away and conferred with his boss. Then I saw the head mobster stand up and walk in my direction.

"Oh no, what are we going to do now?" I muttered to Florence under my breath.

The gangster arrived at our table and asked politely, "May I sit down?"

"Sure," I replied.

"Dr. Calabrese, I owe you a favor," he said.

"Consider it paid," I answered nervously and dug into my ravioli.

"No, hear me out," he continued. "When I was a little boy, my father was out of work. We were on relief in Brooklyn. I was walking around in the snow with holes in my shoes and my feet were soaked. Your father took me into his shoe store, dried my feet, and gave me new socks and new boots. He said, 'Don't tell your father about this.' "

By now I was listening intently because

I knew my father had done this sort of thing for numerous kids in the neighborhood during the Depression. His generosity was one of the reasons that we didn't always know if we would have enough money to pay the next electricity bill.

"I'm going to give you this number — my number," the man said. "If there's ever anything you need — *anything* — don't hesitate to call on me."

Before I could respond he was walking back to his own table. I had stopped chewing my ravioli, and with a half-full mouth I sat there and stared at the number. When I got home that night, I pulled the number out again and looked at it. The man's words raced through my mind — "if there's ever anything you need — *anything* . . ." If I killed the person who was hurting my loved one, I would probably be caught. But if a professional hit man killed him, I wouldn't have anything to worry about.

I picked up the telephone and slowly dialed the number. As the phone rang, my eyes wandered idly over the bookshelf in front of me. A gruff voice answered, "Yes?" on the other end of the line just as my gaze fell on a book that I hadn't thought much about during the past ten years. It was the Bible. Mechanically, I hung up the phone.

What's happening to me? I wondered. How could I even consider plotting murder and putting myself in debt to a leader of organized crime? If I had taken that extra small step — identified myself on that telephone and told the man what I wanted — I would have begun an entirely new evil existence. But the sight of that Bible had triggered a nearly submerged value system that my parents and priests had built into me during my youth. My father never hit anybody. My mother had reiterated, "You don't hurt people, Al." Nuns had taught me, "Thou shalt not kill." One had made me write a thousand lines of "Education begins with self-control," when I had compulsively yelled out something in school.

This structure of values — or "superego," to use Freudian terminology — restrained me from taking out a murder contract on a man that I had grown to hate. But I knew I needed something more than parentally imposed values. I needed something eternally vital, something that would give my life an ultimate meaning and direction. The next time, I realized, my fragile, hard-pressed system of morality might not hold up without some kind of solid support, some convincing reason for following traditional values.

My conscious reason for going to hear Billy Graham was that I wanted to hand out a questionnaire for a research paper. But perhaps, deep inside, I sensed that the message he was preaching might be the ultimate answer I was looking for. I couldn't admit that to my wife or kids. I couldn't even admit it to myself. But God's Spirit had been moving me, talking to me through my patients and my increasing dissatisfaction with my work and my personal life. As Graham spoke that night, he provided, as I said, that last grain of precipitate, that final key word that prompted me to accept Christ as my personal Saviour and allow Him to change my life completely.

As Florence, the seven kids, and I stood up there at the front of Madison Square Garden and committed ourselves to Jesus, a peace and joy that I had never experienced before swept over me. I felt as though my entire previous life had been a distasteful, arduous journey, and now I had finally reached the comfort of home. This sense of complete peace was momentary, however, for the testing soon began.

We had broken up into small groups to talk with counselors, but Florence poked me in the ribs. "Al, Eileen's not here! Where is she?"

Our eleven-year-old daughter had been with us as we walked up to make our commitment, but somehow she had gotten lost in the shuffle. We looked around frantically and couldn't find her anywhere. Some of the crusade officials organized a search party, and people walked around with bull horns shouting, "Eileen Calabrese! Eileen Calabrese!" But still, no Eileen.

How could God allow something like

this to happen? I wondered. Terrible thoughts began to race through my mind — she might have been abducted . . . or injured . . . or . . . Then a woman called us over and said, "Let's all get together and pray for Eileen's safe return." She offered a brief prayer, and then Florence yelled, "Now, let's *look* and pray!" and the search started again in earnest. The prayer helped calm me down, and soon we saw our lost daughter being led toward us by an official.

"Where were you?" I asked, too relieved to think of scolding her.

"Daddy, you said if we were separated, we'd meet at the ticket booth outside in the lobby. When I got lost, I just went out there to wait for you."

That was the first test of my new faith — a small test, but still an important one to prepare me for the really tough trials that were to come later. As we walked toward the exit, the woman counselor asked, "By the way, Dr. Calabrese, what exactly do you to for a living — practice medicine?"

"No," I replied. "I'm a psychoanalyst."

She smiled slightly and then asked, "What are you going to do now?"

"What do you mean?"

"I mean now that you're a Christian, what work are you going to do?" She couldn't conceive that a real Christian could continue to be a Freudian analyst, and I wasn't sure I could either.

I thought for a moment and replied, "I don't know. But I do know I'm going to do what Jesus wants me to do."

Her question stayed in my mind as we drove home that evening. It had never occurred to me that I might be in a profession that was basically inconsistent with the Christian faith. Certainly Freud himself was an atheist, and there is an assumption in Freudian psychoanalysis that there is no God. But did that mean that as a believer I should abandon all Freud's insights about human development? Or was it possible for the light of Christ to transform my practice into an approach to personal relationships that could glorify God? These were questions that still bothered me as I woke up the next morning and prepared to board that depressed hospital ward, the Long Island Rail Road.

Chapter Two

Confessions
of a Closet Christian

The morning after the experience at the Billy Graham rally, my first patient was a woman whose main characteristic was that she talked incessantly. She was a student analyst who had to be psychoanalyzed herself in what we call "didactic analysis," and she participated in the sessions much more than most of my other patients. I had once joked with her by saying I was going to buy a whistle and blow it to stop her from talking long enough for me to make an interpretation of her problems.

But on this particular morning, she was unusually quiet. I initiated the discussion, but I noticed she was only answering in monosyllables.

"You know, this is unlike you to be so

quiet," I said. "Is something bothering you?"

"There's something different about you today," she replied.

"What do you mean?"

She stared at me for a moment and then asked, "Have you become a Christian?"

I was floored. I had said nothing about my personal beliefs or my activities the night before. Apparently in some unconscious, nonverbal way I had communicated my inner transformation to her and I was shocked that she had perceived my experience so accurately.

"Well," I stammered, "I've had a religious experience of sorts." Then I quickly changed the subject and went on the attack to cover my discomfort. "But why did you react to me differently today? Is it threatening to you that I may have had some kind of a religious encounter?"

Discussing my new faith, especially with a fellow professional, made me quite uncomfortable. Like most of my colleagues, this woman was an agnostic who looked with disdain on religion, and I was afraid her talkative nature would prompt her to go out and blab indiscriminately about my conversion experience. If I had told other psychoanalysts, "I've accepted Jesus Christ as my Lord and Saviour," many of them would have responded, "This guy has gone off his rocker."

An analyst is subject to all kinds of analysis on the part of his colleagues. If you have a stomach problem, for example, you have to keep it a deep, dark secret. Otherwise, someone will whisper, "he's internalizing anxiety," or "what incredible rage and hostility that man is repressing." Someone has said that the only thing a psychoanalyst is allowed to die of without being analyzed by his colleagues is getting hit with a truck which has mounted a curb and struck him in his back yard where he's reading a book on Freud on Sunday morning.

So beginning with my first patient, I in effect denied Christ in public. For the first year of my new-born life, I played a game with Him. I prayed, *You created us Lord, so you know what a person like me is exposed to. You know I have to operate with an interior devotion to you. I love you, but I can't make a decent living if I'm too open about it.*

My decision to be a secret, or "closet" Christian also applied to my relations with my Italian-American relatives. I knew if I told them I had attended a Billy Graham meeting, much less walked forward at the evangelist's invitation, they would say I had betrayed my Catholic heritage. Actually, what I would really be doing was betraying Italian cultural traditionalism. They would interpret my commitment as a rejection of them and of their struggle to overcome prejudice and succeed in America. But when I began attending a Protestant church which had a good Bible study program so that I could get a more solid grounding in the Scriptures, word of my activities somehow leaked back to a stern, elderly aunt of mine. She called me in for an audience.

With masterful manipulation, she looked me in the eye and said, "I had an awful dream. Tell me it's not true."

"What's that?" I asked innocently,

dreading what I suspected might be coming.

"I dreamed you were going to a Protestant church. Tell me it's not true."

No slouch at manipulation myself, I sidestepped her question: "Auntie, let me tell you one thing. I love Jesus Christ with all my heart and soul, and I love Him more today than I ever have before. I'm a Christian."

But she wouldn't be put off. "Don't give me that Christian baloney!" she shot back. "Are you a Catholic?"

I told her that I had been out of the Catholic Church for all practical purposes before my experience at the Graham rally. It would have been only a matter of time before all my church ties would have been severed. I also said that although I had tried a couple of churches, I didn't know at that point which denomination I would finally choose. The important thing to me was not the denomination, but my relationship to God. My answer hardly satisfied her, and I was relieved when the discussion was finished and I was back outside in the fresh air. I could see that the best approach to the Christian faith would be to keep my mouth shut tighter than ever so that I could avoid any further unpleasant confrontations.

But this decision to be silent bothered me. In my Bible reading, I kept coming across passages like Paul's statement in 1 Corinthians 4:10: "Here we are, fools for the sake of Christ . . ." This thought became especially unsettling as I continued to run into a man who walked up and down midtown Manhattan with a sandwich board sign which said on the front, "I AM A FOOL FOR CHRIST'S SAKE," and on the back, "WHO'S FOOL ARE YOU?"

Yes, I thought, whose fool *am* I? The people in my profession had shamelessly offered the world some of the most lunatic philosophies imaginable. At psychoanalytic conventions I was always running into psychiatrists from California who wore long saffron robes and flowers in their hair. My cousin Rudy, who had joined me in practice, went up to one man who had a chrysanthemum in one ear and asked with a straight face, "Are you married on that side?" There were also the "lovers," the analysts who went around hugging and kissing everybody. They were jokingly said to spend most of their time throwing paper airplanes from their windows with the message, "Whoever finds this, I love you," written on the wings.

These people are not ashamed of looking foolish, and they had nothing to offer the world in comparison to the truth I had discovered. It was at a convention of the American Academy of Psychotherapists in Miami, with all these lunatic types in the profession flitting about me, that a decisive change occurred in my closet Christian experience.

At this convention, as with most other gatherings of psychotherapists, the divisions and rivalries between different schools of thought ran deep. You'd find an orthodox Freudian who wouldn't talk to a neo-Freudian. The touch and encounter therapists would disdain the behaviorists, and primal screamers howled that they were the only ones with the key to emotional health. But there was one thing that they all had in common on the day that the convention opened: a tremendous respect for Dr. John Rosen, the keynote speaker and founder of the concept of direct psychoanalysis. His pioneering efforts in the field were legendary. While working at a New York hospital, he decided that the usual methods of treating hopeless schizophrenics, including shock therapy and isolated hospitalization, were archaic and primitive. He believed that the best way to deal with these people was to show them love and to become, in effect, a real mother to them. He began to feed, bathe, and dress the hopelessly insane patients, and he would read children's stories to them and tuck them into bed.

Authorities at the hospital told him either to follow the philosophy of the staff administration or leave, so he complied with their rules during daytime. But at night he slipped into the ward and continued to care for these patients with the compassionate approach he was developing. His tremendous success catapulted him to a leading position in the field and he became the leader of the new school of thought, which was dubbed "direct psychoanalysis."

Thunderous applause greeted him as he stood up to deliver the keynote in Miami that year. He proceeded to astound the entire audience, including me, with a speech that was almost a sermon. "We have *failed,*" he declared, and immediately set himself in opposition to most keynote addresses, which stress the positive things that have been accomplished. "We've failed to achieve success with our patients, failed to help them. We've lobotomized, lobectomized, caseworked, proofworked them. But we've lost our way and failed. I've retraced my steps to where I lost my way, and my journey leads me back two thousand years to a man named Jesus Christ."

As he paused, there was dead silence. I couldn't believe my ears.

"I'm not telling you to go out and join a church because I don't know what church to tell you to join," he continued. "I don't know the full theological and philosophical import of what I'm saying. But I do know if we are to reach the people we work with, we psychotherapists have to become more Christ-like.''

He got a standing ovation at the end of his speech. As the significance of his words sank into my mind, I began to feel as though a bombshell had flattened me.

When the applause died down, an ex-priest who was standing next to me asked, ''Isn't John Rosen *Jewish?*''

''Yes,'' I replied, ''but you know, God has been known to speak through Jews before.''

I did a lot of thinking during the remainder of that first session, and when Rudy and I returned to our room, I couldn't hold my feelings back any longer. ''Rudy,'' I said, ''I'm ashamed of myself. Here I am — I've been given grace by God. And here's a man, Rosen, who hasn't even accepted Jesus as his Saviour. Yet he's witnessing more effectively than I ever imagined possible. The Holy Spirit is working through this man, and I'm ashamed of the number of times I could have witnessed to other therapists myself, but didn't.''

Rudy, who had accepted Christ shortly after my own conversion, agreed. ''I guess the time *has* come for us to speak out," he said. "What are you going to do?"

I still hadn't settled on a definite plan, so I decided to play it safe. "I'll tell you what: I'm going to make a promise. If I'm asked to give a keynote address, I'll come out for Jesus Christ."

To a stranger, this might have sounded like a courageous stand. But even though Rudy was too kind to remind me, we both knew that in the forty-six years of my life I had never even been asked to give the keynote address at a Boy Scout meeting. But God won't be kept waiting. Two weeks after we had returned home from the convention, the Society of Clinical Social Workers wrote me a letter: "We would like for you to give the keynote address at our meeting at the Barbizon Plaza. . . ." The Lord was in effect saying to me, "I gotcha, Al!"

Since Rudy knew about my promise and also about the invitation to speak at the hotel in Manhattan, I couldn't very well back out. As I stood up before hundreds of social workers at the Barbizon, I half expected them to jeer, throw ash trays at me, or simply walk out. But I went ahead with my speech as planned. First of all I discussed a few salient facts about the history of psychotherapy. Then I said, "I've learned a great deal from the various philosophers and scientists whose work I've studied and also from my professors who taught me the techniques of psychoanalysis. I'm very grateful for the training I've received. But now I've come to the conclusion that there's another dimension to my life and work that my professors never taught me. I have recently accepted Jesus Christ as my Lord and Saviour and I intend for my career to move in a direction that will be pleasing to Him."

I had finally done it. After convincing myself that I'd never be able to operate both as an effective therapist and an open, professing Christian, I was finally bringing those two parts of my life together. And the ceiling hadn't caved in on me, either. Then my speech seemed to get out of hand. It wasn't that I was incoherent. On the contrary, I was almost *too* coherent. But I was saying things I hadn't planned to say. "I'm thinking about forming some sort of institute which will be dedicated to a synthesis of Christianity and mental health," I said. "It will probably be a training institute, in addition to a treatment center."

When I had finished, the audience, to my surprise, actually applauded enthusiastically. One of my former professors hurried up to the front and hugged me on the podium. "I understand what you're trying to do," she said.

There was some negative reaction, but the naysayers were in a distinct minority. I had weathered the most difficult task of my career and had come out much stronger for the experience. *Why didn't I do this the day after the Graham rally?* I asked myself. It had been relatively easy, and now I could live my life as a whole, an integrated entity which included both my faith and my profession.

Standing up openly for Christ was not always the easiest thing, however. I recall my wife telling me one evening that she really wanted a stereo for the house.

"I don't have the money right now

because I've got to pay the taxes," I said. "Let's wait a few months and see then."

She agreed, but I hated to turn her down. I knew she and the kids would enjoy listening to a good stereo system. The next morning, I got a call out of the blue from a man who said, "Doc, you don't know me, but I know you. I have a couple of stereos that go for about fifteen hundred dollars apiece, but I can let you have one for three hundred. What do you say?"

"What's the story?" I asked.

"Don't ask what the story is. They're brand new, packed."

"Why are they so cheap?" I insisted.

"Don't ask any questions. Just tell me where to send one."

It was beginning to dawn on me that Satan, as well as God, works in wondrous ways. "No, I can't take it," I said. "If I did, it would undo everything I'm trying to accomplish in my life because I've become a Christian."

"Are you crazy?" the man cried. "This is fifteen hundred dollars I'm talking about!"

"No, absolutely not."

Bewildered, he finally hung up but I

think I got my point across. I felt a certain exhilaration inside because now I knew where I was going and what I stood for. But plenty of rough spots and pitfalls were waiting for me on this open road for Christ that I had chosen.

Even though I had become a committed Christian, I still enjoyed the family festivities that are a part of every Italian's heritage. One of our customs was to have a gathering of our extended family — cousins, aunts, uncles — on the Fourth of July. Our home on Long Island was a natural setting for a family picnic because of our extra land. We were enjoying heaps of good Italian food and music when a neighbor of mine stormed over and shouted, "Calabrese, this is it! We're not going to stand for any more of those fireworks you people are shooting off!"

As a matter of fact, we weren't shooting off any fireworks, and I told him so, but he refused to believe me. One thing led to another, and he finally threatened to call the police.

"Look, I've tried to be reasonable with you!" I yelled. "Now I'm going to give you five seconds to get off my property!"

The man's wife, who had followed him over, retorted, "I feel like taking a swing at you, you jerk!"

"If you take a swing at me, you're no longer a lady, and I'm going to act like man-to-man and flatten you!" I shouted.

They soon left in a huff without any blows being traded, but afterward, when I calmed down, the incident began to weigh on my mind. "What would Jesus do if he were in my shoes now?" I asked. Even though I didn't know this neighbor well, I liked what I had seen of him before our argument. I had even given him a ride into the city within the past month. As a Christian, I knew I had no choice except to try to repair the friendship.

The next day, which was a Sunday, seemed to be the proper time to straighten things out. I bought a small gift and walked over to the man's house. Holding the peace offering out to him, I said, "I'm really sorry for what I said yesterday, and I'd like for us to continue to be friends."

He melted before my eyes and seemed so grateful and happy. He knew of my

Christian orientation, and my gesture was important to show him that I believed in living my faith as well as talking about it.

As my reputation as a serious, rather than just a cultural Christian came to be known around the neighborhood, some people began to come over for informal counseling. The fact that I was a psychoanalyst gave me an aura of expertise, but that hadn't been enough to attract them in the past. Somehow, the focus on Jesus was changing my relations with others by making me more approachable, especially to those whose emotional problems had a spiritual dimension.

One man who had never deigned to speak to me before, called late one evening and said it was very important for him to discuss something with me. He came over a few minutes later, and I asked, "Why are you so interested in talking to me in particular?"

"You're the only one I can talk to as a Christian," he replied. "I don't understand you exactly, I mean, the kind of Christianity you're into. But I somehow feel I can talk to you."

We discussed his personal problem from 1:00 A.M. to 5:00 A.M., and I described to him, as best I could, how he could relate to God through Christ and apply his faith in resolving his difficulty. As the first rays of the sun began to stream through my living room window, he sighed, leaned back, and said, "You know, I take my reputation in my hands by talking to you."

"What do you mean?" I asked.

"Well, not everybody is as broad-minded as I am."

"I still don't get you."

"I mean the fact that you're an Italian. Italians are not acceptable to many of the people I associate with, you know."

Before I became a Christian, I would have given him a good Italian punch for a remark like that. But this time I just smiled and tried my best to understand what was making the guy tick. He headed wearily for his own home shortly afterward, and, although he never visited me again, I make it a point to keep in touch with him through friendly little gestures such as Christmas cards and occasional gifts.

It was interesting for me, a professional psychotherapist, to observe the change in my own ability to relate to others. My inner hostilities, defense mechanisms, and personal weaknesses were being healed by Christ's love. It was inevitable that this transformation would bring about a radical alteration in my professional life. I began to see the potential of applying a firm Christain faith to the problems of some of my patients, whose primary difficulties might be related to finding the meaning of life.

The first step in bringing Christ into the psychoanalytic field was to set up the Christian institute I had mentioned in my keynote address to the social workers. I wanted to hang on to my Park Avenue practice because it was established and lucrative. But an increasing number of ministers began to refer patients to me, and the double workload in Manhattan and Long Island began to get out of hand. My cousin Rudy and I discussed Scripture on our lunch hours and talked about how we could best serve Christ in our profession.

"I think we should start the institute right away, and it seems to me the best place to do that will be out on Long Island," I told him. "The only choice I can see we have is to close down the Park Avenue office and focus on Long Island, where we'll be able to set up a teaching program and do community work, as well as treat patients."

It was a frightening prospect for both of us because most of our income — about 60 per cent of it — came from our Park Avenue office. We would have to give up referral sources that had taken years to establish. We'd have to say good-by both to five-course meals in the best Manhattan restaurants and also to our respected status and regular relationships with very important people. I had even become something of a guru among therapists who had been my students and moved on to their own practices. All this would have to go if we decided to set up the Long Island institute, but I told Rudy I felt strongly that God was leading me in this direction.

He thought for a moment and then with

a chuckle asked, "Are you sure God knows what He's doing?"

He agreed to join me, and we moved into a small office in Merrick on Long Island and then switched to larger offices in Hicksville. My income dropped almost immediately by 50 per cent, and that hurt. It hurt even more when some non-Christian colleagues started whispering behind my back, "Calabrese has got a gimmick with this Christian thing. He's really raking in the money." Nothing could have been further from the truth, as both Rudy's family and mine will attest, but these therapists couldn't understand any motive other than money.

Even though our personal income remained lower than it had been, God soon provided us with more patients than we could handle by ourselves. We increased our staff steadily until at this writing we have twenty therapists at the institute. As one of our analysts has quipped, "Our couches are never cool." The fact that we called our organization the "Christian Institute for Psychotherapeutic Studies" has encouraged many believers to come to us for counseling. More than half of our new clients were committed Christians or people who had a Christian background and were looking for spiritual as well as emotional help. Unlike many secular psychoanalytic centers, a Christian could come to us and know his faith was not going to be treated as a part of his illness.

As I was relaxing after supper one evening, I found myself evaluating the spiritual journey I had been taking during the past couple of years. My life had turned around completely at the Billy Graham rally. John Rosen's keynote address had pushed me out of my spiritual closet and encouraged me to go public with my faith. My psychoanalytic practice had also undergone a conversion because Jesus Christ and His love now had a prominent part in my approach to therapy. But something was still not quite right. The problem, I realized, was that I hadn't found a permanent church home, a spiritual environment where I could find solid fellowship and still feel comfortable, socially and culturally.

I had enjoyed going to several evangelical Protestant churches and had learned a great deal about Scripture, which had not been stressed at some Roman Catholic churches I had attended. But I missed the rich, liturgical tradition of the Catholic Mass and the religious customs and observances that were a distinctive part of my Italian-American heritage. During Lent, for example, the church altar would be draped in purple, the color of mourning, in anticipation of the crucifixion of Christ. Then on Good Friday, the altar would be stripped bare, and the gate to the altar would be left open to symbolize Christ's death. The next day, Holy Saturday, the church would be darkened and just before midnight three Masses would be conducted. When midnight arrived and Easter Sunday began, the lights would go on in the church and the bells would begin to toll to declare that Christ is risen!

I had grown up with these customs and they meant a great deal to me, so I finally decided to try the Roman Church again. I knew I couldn't return to it on the same terms that I had left, because Jesus was a real, living person to me now. Before, He had been a dying, stagnant part of a cultural tradition. Afraid that I would feel completely out of place as a Catholic, I half expected to end up as a man without a church, a believer who didn't fit into any denominational niche. I had no notion that I would discover in that old liturgical context a dimension of God's Spirit that would give me inner power as a Christian that I had never believed possible.

Chapter Three

A New Kind of Healing

My first attempt to re-enter the Roman Catholic Church was almost a disaster. I'm a member of a Catholic laymen's organization, and I decided it would be easier for me to get involved in the Church again through this group, rather than by just attending Mass. There were more than two hundred people at the meeting, and I became thoroughly disillusioned after about five minutes. Most of the members seemed uninterested in talking with me. Those I did strike up conversations with appeared to have no understanding of the kind of Christian faith that I had acquired.

By all outward appearances I fit in as "Brother Francis Xavier" — my two middle names which I had always used at the group's gatherings in the past. But I knew that I had completely lost contact with the kind of cultural Catholicism I saw around me. I felt like a stranger and wondered if there was even one person present who would identify with my story. The worst loneliness is being in a group — especially a religious group — where everyone but you is relating to someone else. Feeling totally isolated and rejected, I finished my coffee and turned to leave. But just then a man tapped me on the shoulder and said, "Excuse me, my name is Vinnie. Something inside me said I should walk over and talk to you."

"What made you pick me out of all these people?" I asked, gesturing around the room.

"A feeling inside just said, 'Tell that man your story,'" he replied. "I'm a charismatic Catholic, and I've learned to respond to God's Spirit under some of the most unlikely circumstances — such as right now."

"What do you mean, 'charismatic'?" I asked.

"It's a movement in the different

Christian churches — both Catholic and Protestant — where there's an emphasis on moving with the Holy Spirit and exercising the gifts He has given us."

Vinnie's story, as it turned out, was almost the same as mine — reaction to the Catholic Church, Bible study in Protestant denominations, and a return to the Catholic tradition because of a need for the Roman style of worship.

By the time he had finished, I was totally enthralled. "I don't want to let you go," I said.

"Why don't you come to a meeting we have out at Molloy College in Rockville Centre?" he suggested.

We set up a time to meet outside the college the following week, and then I headed for home. Almost as soon as I had left Vinnie, though, I began to have reservations. The group he belonged to sounded rather unusual, and I was already enough of an outcast in my family and among my professional colleagues without going completely off the deep end. But I was hungry for fellowship, and the idea of finding Catholics who believed the way I did, even if they were a bit kooky, was too appealing to miss. When I met Vinnie at Molloy College, we walked into the cafeteria, where about sixty men and women, mostly lay people, were milling around talking to one another. I felt rather apprehensive because I didn't know what was coming next. I had had a patient who was a charismatic, and she had vaguely described something about the movement to me, but I knew I'd have to experience it to understand exactly what it was all about.

Unlike the Catholic laymen's group, the people I met in the college cafeteria were solicitous and friendly. There was a peace, a softness and tenderness about their countenances that indicated they weren't afraid of contact with strangers. Their language was sprinkled with "Praise the Lord!" but I had become used to this way of talking in my experience with evangelical Protestant churches.

The thing I wasn't quite prepared for was the meeting that followed. We arranged our chairs in a large circle and after we sat down, a nun, who seemed to be the leader of the group, began to pray spontaneously. Several people held their hands in the air, with their palms up, and I thought they looked a little out of it. The prayers continued with different men and women in the room participating, and there were interjections of "Praise God!" "Praise Jesus!" "Glory!" "Amen!" "Praise that name!" "Jesus, we thank you!"

Then a meek, shy man whom I had met earlier in the evening, boomed forth in an authoritative, decisive voice: "My children, I would that you would listen to my will for you this evening. . . ." I could hardly believe that the man who was speaking now was the same one who had been stammering and blushing before me earlier. At first I wondered, *What is this guy doing?* Then, I realized I had heard a prophecy because he was speaking in the first person, as though it were God Himself giving us guidance.

When he had finished, there was a wave of "Praise Him!" "Alleluia!" "Praise Him!"

The turn that the meeting had taken

was bothering me by now, but the biggest shock came when a man on the other side of the room began to babble strange sounds. My eyes cut around toward him and I wondered if he was having a seizure. But the sounds were too controlled and directed for that. Then I realized he must be speaking in tongues. Although I had heard of this phenomenon, I had hardly expected to witness it firsthand. His words had an ancient, Middle-Eastern sound, and the whole effect was quite eerie. I began to wonder seriously what I was doing there because I was sure this was not my kind of worship experience. But my attitude changed dramatically as someone in the group began to hum and the whole room broke forth into a beautiful crescendo of sound. A majority of the people were singing in tongues, and each of the prayer languages was different; miraculously, though, the result was completely harmonious.

As the strange, exotic song began to die down, I realized that there was a thread that had been running through the entire meeting, even though I had thought at first there was no rhyme or reason to it. This simple but comforting theme was that God was present with those at that meeting and would continue to be present after we broke up and went our separate ways. Nothing had been planned beforehand, but someone who had perceived the spiritual thread during the meeting mentioned it.

This free group worship experience was part of what Vinnie had originally described to me as "moving with the Spirit." I was beginning to see what he was getting at now. As a committed Christian, I could just relax and let God's Spirit work through me and in me, whether in a meeting like this or in my daily job and family life. He could heal my own emotional wounds — as He had done on a number of occasions since the Graham crusade — and He could use me to help heal other people. The important thing was for me to submit to Him completely and not get in His way by trying to control my own life and my relationships with others.

The tongues and the prophecies seemed

more palatable as this insight swept over me. I could tell these people were having a genuine experience with God; they were relating to Him in ways that I wanted to learn more about. So I accepted an invitation by one of the nuns to attend a seminar on the charismatic movement and the working of the Holy Spirit. During the next eight weeks, I listened to the scriptural evidence for speaking in tongues. The Apostle Paul, I learned, was quite straightforward about the subject: ". . . I should like you all to have the gift of tongues, . . ." (1 Corinthians 14: 5). By opening myself up more to the Holy Spirit, I could enhance the gifts I already possessed and might also receive additional spiritual gifts.

To show that I wanted the Spirit to come down upon me and use me, I submitted to a laying on of hands at the end of the course. About eight people put their hands on my head and shoulders, and one person prayed. Then someone said, "Speak with your new tongue!"

I didn't feel like speaking in a strange tongue at the time, and I refused to contrive that sort of thing. I didn't want to go along with anything that smacked of phoniness. But I did feel unusually comfortable and warmly emotional as they prayed over me. After this experience, I sensed a new freedom in my relationship with God, a freedom to do whatever moved me.

This freedom in the Spirit found its first expression in little things, such as casual encounters with strangers. I remember when I was standing near the religious section in a bookstore on Long Island, a woman walked up to me and pointed to a symbol of the Holy Spirit that I wore as a lapel pin. "What's that?" she asked. When I told her, she said, "I'd like to buy one myself. Where did you get it?"

I told her of a shop a short distance away that carried them. Then on second thought I took the pin off, placed it in the palm of her hand, and made a sign of the cross over it.

"What's your name?" I asked.

"Norma," she replied.

"Norma, I'll pray for you," I told her, and she immediately broke down and began to cry.

"Thank you, thank you," she murmured.

That's something I would never have done before I started learning to respond freely to God's Spirit. It was a nonrational act on my part — not irrational or against reason, but outside the normal rational processes. It was not something a dignified, conventional person would have done. But I somehow felt the Spirit prodding me, so I moved with God and it was precisely the right thing to do.

My growing sense of freedom with God eventually led me into that experience that had always made me suspicious — speaking in tongues. During private prayer one evening, I felt a tremendously warm, loving feeling toward God, and ordinary words seemed inadequate to express this sense that welled up inside me. Strange sounds — some unknown, guttural language — poured forth from my lips, and my communication with God somehow felt more complete than it ever had before.

This experience recurs periodically when

I feel a great sense of enthusiasm or overwhelming love because of the way I've seen God act in my life. I've decided it's an ability that God gives us to enhance our capacity to celebrate Him. I read somewhere that every animal has a distinguishable noise of celebration. Human beings also have distinctive noises of joy for different occasions. When one person is at a baseball game and his favorite player hits a home run with the bases loaded, the fan may jump up and shout "Yahoo!" This is a nonrational expression of inner ecstasy that ordinary language cannot match. Speaking in tongues serves the same function for me.

I was walking along Jones Beach on the southern coast of Long Island by myself one evening, enjoying the sound of the waves washing up on the shore and the sight of fish jumping out of the water. Night had just fallen, and the first stars were beginning to twinkle in the clear sky. I realized all at once that I was the only human on the beach, and I was struck with the thought of how small I was in this tremendous universe. I was not even equal to a grain of sand on that beach in terms of the number of stars and constellations above me. But how infinitely more gifted I was than any of those heavenly bodies! The Lord had made me aware of their existence, while they lacked any awareness of themselves or of me. A warm feeling toward God welled up inside me. Words were inadequate to express what I felt. I couldn't even say something in Italian and convey the depths of my emotion. My prayer language, the strange, untranslatable tongue, rolled off my lips and enabled me to release the love I felt.

This inner sense of spiritual freedom became especially important when tragedy struck my family one Christmas season. My sister's husband, a Lutheran who had become a Catholic, died of a massive cerebral hemorrhage at the age of forty-six, and left behind a wife and eight children who loved him dearly. My sister Frances called me from the hospital to tell me about the attack, and I rushed over, only to find that a machine was all that was keeping Dick's bodily functions going. The doctor who had been attending him pulled me aside and said, "You just tell me when you want me to turn off the switch. There aren't any brain waves. Technically, he's dead."

I told Frances and the kids, and one of his daughters, who always called me by my nickname, "Freddie," threw herself at me and cried, "Uncle Freddie, please don't!" She held onto my legs and waist, as tears streamed down her cheeks.

Even the young nurses around us were crying. Dick had been such a beautiful, religious person, so kind and so handsome.

Frances said, "There's my life," as she pointed toward the hospital room where Dick lay. "Thank you, God, for a beautiful life. It was such a beautiful thing. I knew it couldn't last."

I gathered the family together and said, "Let's go down to the lobby." We retired to a quiet corner, and I said, "Now first of all, let's praise God and thank Him, even for this. We're not born into this life, but into eternity. Realize one thing, children, we all have this appointment to keep. We're standing here in this hospital, but only a short time ago in the history of our universe Indians were running around in this very place. A short time later an archaeologist may be digging through the wreckage of this hospital. So let's praise God and thank Him because we have faith, even though we don't always understand. This is our opportunity to say, 'We trust you, Lord and believe in you, even in this terrible moment.' "

To my surprise, the kids immediately said, "Thank you, God, thank you, Jesus, thank you."

The funeral was scheduled for Christmas Eve, and take it from me, a funeral parlor is the loneliest place to be at that time. We could hear happy sleighbells ringing outside, and to make it even worse, there was a bar and grill across the street. As our family gathered in the little funeral chapel, the drunken conversation and singing drifted over from the bar, with the drunks slurring, "Chrish ish born in Bethlehem . . ."

To top it all off, the priest who conducted the service pulled our spirits down to rock bottom. In a perfunctory, callous way, he stood up at the front and said gruffly, "All right, just kneel down there and we'll say one decade of the rosary." He obviously wanted to get back to his own Christmas Eve celebration. In a rote, prayer-wheel style that turns my stomach, he rattled off the Lord's prayer: "Ourfatherwhoartinheavenhallowedbethy namekingdomJesus . . ." Then, hardly taking a breath, he mumbled, "HailMaryfullofgrace. . . ." Before I knew what had happened, he spat out, "Where's the family?" walked over to them, shook hands, and was out of the door.

I walked slowly over to the bier, put my hand on it, and said softly, "Dick, you deserved better than that." He *did* deserve more because he had been a good father. Suddenly, I felt an inspiration. Something inside me said, *You give the homily.*

"But they'll think I'm crazy!" I protested to this inner voice.

You give the homily, the feeling insisted.

"What will I talk about?"

Just get up there and say "uhh" and you'll start talking.

I'd never tried anything like that before, and if I had not had other unusual experiences with God's Spirit, I would have shrugged off this inclination as some sort of aberration. My reservations kept holding me back: "Gee, they'll think I'm really whacked out," I thought. "My sisters — I don't know how they'll accept something like that from me. And my wife and other relatives are here."

I turned around and faced the others and was on the verge of not saying anything. But I muttered an "uhh," and then realized I had to keep going and deliver whatever the Spirit wanted to me to say, or split. The words that came out were more appropriate than anything I could have prepared.

"Here we are on Christmas Eve, and you may be asking what we're doing in a funeral parlor on a day like this," I began. "Why did God do this to us? Is this all there is to it? Is this the end of Richard?

"You know, we're here crying for him, but we're crying for ourselves too because we have to spend Christmas Eve in a funeral parlor. No one wants to be in a place like this on such a festive day. In the distance, we can hear the strains of happiness from the tavern across the road. From the inn. The inn. You know, maybe God wants us to understand the loneliness of the Holy Family on that Christmas Eve long ago. They may have heard the same strains of drunken joy from their inn. They were alone in a stable, but they had more in that humble manger than the people in the inn who were singing. They had a love that bound them together, and the joy of knowing that the Messiah had come. Even at that moment of lonely, painful childbirth, people were being informed of the coming of the Christ. That was love. Let's let love tie us together tonight. We have people from many denominations here — Catholic, Lutheran, Baptist — but that's not important. The important thing is that our hearts and minds are made for God."

I spoke to them from the heart, and they were moved. The Spirit also began to move among the children. Two of Dick's sons came up to me and asked, "Do you mind if we read something from the Scriptures?"

I knew they hadn't been trained too thoroughly in the Bible, but I told them to find a passage they wanted to read. They went into the waiting room and returned shortly, saying, "Uncle Freddie, would this be a good thing to read?"

What did they pick out? The passage from the Gospel of John that described how Jesus raised his friend Lazarus from the dead. "That's beautiful," I said. "How did you pick that out?"

The older boy said, "I opened the Bible, and there it was."

"Well, the Lord moved you," I told him. "You get up there and you read that."

So the kids put a little program together. Some of the adults protested at first: "No, now this is just not done!"

But I said, "They want to do it, and God is leading them to do it. Those are beautiful Bible readings, and it's only right that this man's sons should give them."

That Christmas Eve was one of the

most significant experiences of my life because I saw what incredible things the Spirit of God could do if I would only open myself up and allow Him to guide me. And if the Spirit could produce such positive, loving results in a tense, sad family situation, why couldn't He operate in the same way in my dealings with patients?

Most Freudian psychoanalysts would immediately launch into a good belly laugh at the idea of using prayer in a therapy session. But the freedom that God had given me opened up this possibility in my dealings with my patients. One Christian woman, June, came to me with a terrible marital problem. Her husband was a very disturbed person, on the verge of psychosis, and his constant abuse made their relationship almost unbearable. She suffered from horrendous nightmares, and would frequently wake up, trying to say some word, but unable to spit it out: "Mmmmmmmm . . ." She would scream and sometimes fall out of her bed during the violent thrashing that gripped her.

As we talked about her difficulty, I

probed into her early family background to try to determine the causes for her problems. It immediately became apparent that she had a serious memory block. She couldn't remember anything that had happened to her before she was eight years old. It's a basic principle of depth psychology that the therapist must learn about the relationship the person had with his mother and father. Because most of our serious adult problems stem from traumatic childhood experiences and relationships, it's important to get the individual to confront and understand his early parental influences so that he can heal his present emotional wounds. The fact that June had allowed herself to be abused by her husband without any protest indicated to me that she probably had developed a personality trait as a child which would have to be changed if she hoped to live a productive adult life.

As with many people who are confronting serious emotional problems, she was re-creating some early childhood experience in an effort to heal her emotions, only to find that in some way she kept repeating the original experience. What was the early trauma that was giving her so much trouble? I had to find that out, so I tried every imaginable Freudian gimmick to pry open her memory — but nothing worked. Her memory had suffered some sort of psychological lesion, as though a destructive force had ripped through her mind and amputated all her early recollections in one swipe. Finally, I gave up, and decided to let God do the work. During the first fifteen years of my practice, I would probably have given up completely on a person like June, but the Holy Spirit freed me to try a new kind of healing.

"I feel moved to pray over you, June, to put my hands on your head and pray," I said. "Would that be all right with you?"

She was at the end of her rope, and she readily agreed. I placed my hands on her head, closed my eyes and said, "Lord, I'm praying over my sister June. Heal her memory. Open up the dam that prevents any early recall from coming through. Let her see that thing she can't remember and help her not to be afraid of it, so that we can move on to other things. Deliver her of the pain that this blockage is causing."

That very night, she had a dream in which she saw herself calling out, "Jesus! Jesus!"

Then Jesus appeared in the dream and walked over to a closet door and opened it. Out fell her third-grade books, the books she had used when she was eight years old. She turned to Jesus in the dream and cried, "Mmmmmmmmmother! Mother! Mother!"

She woke up at that point, and everything began to come back to her. She recalled that when she was eight years old, her father, who had been an alcoholic, had come home drunk late once night, stumbled into her room and jumped on her bed. He had wrapped her blankets around her so that she couldn't move, and she became terrified. June had tried to call her mother, but she was too frightened. Her recollection of that terrible experience opened up the floodgates for all sorts of early memories. She couldn't get her fill in our subsequent sessions of discussing her childhood. And by confronting and understanding the murderous feelings she had felt toward her father during that incident, she was better able to understand her relationship with her husband, who had taken the place of her father in her adult life. She felt tremendous hostility toward her husband. But she had been unwilling to acknowledge this anger because she subconsciously saw him as having stepped into the shoes of the authoritative, abusive, virtually omnipotent father of her childhood.

June was finally able to understand that both her husband and father were men who needed her help and the help of professional therapists. She realized she was no longer a child who had to submit to senseless abuse but was an adult who should deal with her husband as an adult. After acknowledging the murderous feelings she felt toward her husband, she could see that she was now a mature person who could vent justified anger on occasion without having to worry about losing control and killing someone.

The exhilaration I experienced at

witnessing the power of prayer in psychotherapy even encouraged me to pray with my non-Christian clients when the Spirit prompted. One Jewish fellow, Ben, came to me in such a severe state of depression that he was talking about suicide. His father had died a year before, he said, but he couldn't accept the death. He felt guilty about his fights with the old man and had recurrent dreams of his father pulling him into the grave. These experiences frightened him so much that he felt he couldn't go to his synagogue to light a memorial light in honor of the first anniversary of his father's death.

"I don't believe in that tradition anyhow," he rationalized.

"I'm just afraid you're going to feel even more guilty if you don't do it," I said.

"Yes, I know that," he admitted. "But I can't do it."

The Spirit seemed to be moving me, and I said, "I'd like to pray either with you or for you. I'd like to pray you'll be relieved of this depression and fear."

He seemed very grateful that I felt

comfortable in making this suggestion, so I said, "Lord, please open up Ben's heart and let him see himself the way you see him. Remove this sense of despair he has and take away his feelings of guilt. Help him to let his father rest in peace."

I even closed the prayer, "in Jesus' precious name," and when I raised my head, I could see he was touched. The next day at Mass I was inspired to light a candle in memory of Ben's father. I called him up afterward and said, "I lit this candle. I know it's a Christian church, and you're a Jew, but that candle is burning in remembrance of your father."

There was a brief silence on the other end of the line, and then he said, "From now to the day I die, anything you want, you got."

To this day he treats me as a member of his family — all because I offered a prayer and a religious observance which are not supposed to concern Freudian psychoanalysts.

My last shackles of phony psychoanalytic professionalism fell away during a session I had with Margaret, a vivacious young member of the Catholic charismatic movement who was suffering from a tremendous depression. She explained to me that her despair stemmed from an experience she had had with a female friend who had begged Margaret several times to shoot her with a gun. She refused, but her friend killed herself anyhow, and Margaret began to suffer from a tremendous guilt because she thought she might have prevented the suicide.

As I questioned her about the incident, Margaret admitted she had become frustrated with her friend and had even wished secretly that the young woman *would* kill herself so that Margaret wouldn't have to worry about her any more. As we discussed Margaret's early family history, I learned that her parents had been rather indifferent and cold toward her and that she felt they favored her brothers.

"Your guilt about this friend of yours *does* stem from the fact that at one point you wished this young woman would kill herself," I explained. "You felt a degree of hostility toward her — natural hostility, I might add — because she was putting you in a difficult situation. But there's another thing you may not be aware of: When this woman asked you to shoot her, she was being very hostile to herself. The most hostile thing you can do is give a person a gun and say, 'Please kill me,' because you're asking that person to set himself up for a criminal charge and a lifetime of remorse.''

Margaret's depression resulted from the fact that she couldn't bear this sense of guilt, but these feelings had roots in her personality that ran far deeper than her encounter with the suicide. By saying, 'I should have been able to make this girl respect me enough to prevent her from committing suicide,' you're also saying 'I should have done something to get my parents to respect and love me,' '' I told her gently. ''I can detect feelings of hostility you have toward your parents because you think they loved your siblings more than you. In fact, your parents may not have been able to show adequate love to *any* of their children, but it seemed to you they were singling you out."

Margaret said she understood what I was saying and acknowledged the validity of my analysis, but nothing seemed to raise her from her depression. She was also confronting a disturbing vocational crisis because she was trying to choose a career, but she seemed unable to get moving because of the way her depression had immobilized her.

I prayed about her situation, and the answer to the prayer came in a context which would have been the object of my scorn before I became a committed Christian. I attended meetings of some Catholic charismatic groups on Long Island, and decided one evening that I would go to one sponsored by Father Chris Aridas, a good friend who was a leader in the national charismatic movement. The minute I walked into the room where the meeting was being held, I spotted Margaret.

She ran over to me and said, "I didn't know you belonged to this group! I don't want you to think I'm following you around, but this is really a surprise."

I smiled and replied, "That would be something, for you to follow an old fifty-year-old guy like me," and we both had a good laugh. The atmosphere was quite different from the therapy center, but I soon began to see that the potential for emotional healing was as great here as it was in my office. Margaret told Father Aridas about our counseling sessions, and he walked over and said, "I'm going to pray over her, and I'd like for you to join us. What do you think?"

I hesitated for a moment — the old Freudian resistances made me think twice — but then I replied, "I've never heard of it being done — a priest and a psychoanalyst praying over a person — but let's try it!"

We went into an adjoining room with two other mature Christian men, and Margaret knelt as the priest put his hand on her head and I gripped the back of her neck. The other men put their hands on our shoulders. Each of us prayed at length, for about a half hour. The prayers focused on a central theme: "Lord, open up Margaret's heart so that she can see herself the way Jesus sees her. Help her to accept herself and perceive the beauty and worthwhileness in herself. Open up her heart, Lord, so that she can receive the love of those around her."

Margaret finally broke down into convulsive crying, something which she had been unable to do during a half-dozen sessions with me. Tears flowed all around, as though someone had turned on a faucet. At that point, I moved to a new plateau in the freedom I had been developing as a Spirit-filled Christian. Spontaneous prayer, tongues, and especially prophecy had seemed weird and unsophisticated to me when I first encountered the charismatics. But now I felt moved to prophesy myself. God spoke through me in the first person: "My dear Margaret, I have heard your prayer and I want you to be delivered from the oppressiveness of depression and from all things that tie you down and keep you from walking in the ministry that I have planned for you. Free yourself. Put your faith completely in me and move along in that ministry."

The words came out of my mouth spontaneously, in a completely unplanned flow. I didn't think there was anything profound about them, but Margaret smiled with a look of peace that I had never seen on her face before. As we were walking out of the room, I joked, "Do you realize I've made psychoanalytic history tonight? This is the first time in the history of psychotherapy that the therapist has both prayed and prophesied over a patient." We all laughed, and Margaret seemed especially happy.

The next day when she was in my office for a session, she said, "I'm completely relieved today. The depression has left, and I'm more certain of my vocation. At least, I know I'm going to move forward in choosing a line of work and let God guide me in that choice. When you said to walk in God's ministry last night, I got a tremendous amount of meaning out of that. I never thought about a vocation as being a ministry."

Margaret is now pursuing a fulfilling career in social work. During the months that I saw her after that prayer meeting, she never showed any signs of depression again. We were freed to leave her depression behind and move into other areas of her personality that needed healing.

This experience with Margaret was a watershed in my own spiritual development because God showed me that the insights of an atheist like Freud could be modified into a powerful psychoanalytic tool through the working of the Spirit in my life and in the lives of my clients. I feel Freud made many mistakes as he developed and applied his theories. He overemphasized the importance of sex as the basis for human behavior. His own fear of death prevented him from exploring fully man's need for ultimate meaning. Freud himself fainted twice in public — and on both occasions he was discussing death. But his contributions to the understanding of personality development are invaluable and have too often been cast aside by Christian counselors because Freud himself was not a believer.

As a committed Christian, I could now

take what was valid in Freudian psychology and apply it, but without being constricted by the theoretical rigidity that prevents so many psychoanalysts from seeing what is really wrong with a person. Many analysts would scorn the use of prayer or prophecy in a session with a patient, and I would have scoffed myself before my own encounter with Christ. But now I see God's Spirit as the vehicle which can take secular psychoanalytic theory and turn a therapeutic session into a love relationship.

My method, if it can be called that, might be described as a "Christian love treatment" because the Lord has made me concerned with healing in the most complete sense of the word. True healing should repair the wounds in the individual's personality, in his dealings with others, and in his relationship with God. I've seen the Spirit heal my own emotional problems. I've seen Him comfort my clients and coax them out of their depressions, sexual anxieties, and other inner difficulties. I'm convinced that it's quite possible for Christian lay people to help one another in a distinctive way as lay therapists. That's what the rest of this book is all about — the ways in which the Spirit can help you, as a Christian, to apply traditional psychoanalytic techniques to effect a new kind of healing, a powerful Christian love treatment.

Part Two:
THE CHRISTIAN
LOVE TREATMENT

Chapter Four

What Is the Christian Love Treatment?

Everyone has at some point suffered an emotional or psychological wound. Depression, anxiety, sexual malfunctions — the list is as long as our population. You yourself may be confronting some nerve-racking inner problem right now. Perhaps you're worried about your next promotion at work, or you sense life is tasteless, without any meaning. As if your own problems weren't enough, you probably have family members and friends who are wrestling with their peculiar emotional hang-ups. And in the process of trying to solve or escape these difficulties, they're making your life miserable.

An entire industry, which might be dubbed "Psychotherapy Unlimited," has sprung up to treat these emotional ills. Pastors, marriage counselors, psychoanalysts, psychiatrists, and clinical psychologists hardly have to compete for business, so great is the demand for their services. Some serious problems require the professional help these therapists can offer, but many of your emotional difficulties, and those of your loved ones, are within your power to heal if you know how to go about it.

"Psychotherapy" is a broad term that refers to informal counseling as well as professional analysis. If a husband listens to his wife describe her problems with a next-door neighbor, he's doing psychotherapy. Likewise, a husband may drag into the house and say, "Boy, did I have a lousy day!" If his wife guides him to a chair and replies, "Tell me about it, dear," she doing psychotherapy too. The firmest foundation for this emotional dealing is a tremendously potent power source called "love," but the name has been so corrupted by contemporary misuse that I almost hesitated to refer to it.

At a psychoanalytic convention I

attended recently, one of the speakers asked rhetorically, "What is love? The strains of distant violins or the triumphant twang of a bedspring?"

He went on to argue in favor of the bedspring, and I almost got sick. We've lost the real meaning of love and the access to the healing power in human development that accompanies it, and that distresses me. My experience with Christ has taught me that eternal, authentic love involves sacrifice and commitment. Jesus laid down the ultimate standard for this kind of love when he told his disciples, "A man can have no greater love than to lay down his life for his friends." (John 15:13).

Love must be defined by the impact it has on human relationships. If I really love you as a fellow child of God, then I'll do things to help you, to make your life more meaningful. If you need healing, I'll try to provide it for you. If you need comfort, I'll make myself available. If you need money to tide you over, I'll pull out my wallet. The Apostle Paul, perhaps the greatest expert on love after Jesus, stressed the importance of combining a compassionate attitude with a solid commitment to help. "Love is always patient and kind; it is never jealous; love is never boastful or conceited; it is never rude or selfish; it does not take offence, and is not resentful. Love takes no pleasure in other people's sins but delights in the truth; it is always ready to excuse, to trust, to hope, and to endure whatever comes." (1 Corinthians 13:4 - 7).

If you can grasp the love that Jesus and Paul described and allow the Spirit of Christ to channel it through you to others, you will gain access to a force for healing emotional wounds and interpersonal relationships that will know no limits. I know the power is there because I've seen it and experienced it. As you know from the first section of this book, I lived without that spiritual power source for fourty-six years, until Jesus converted me from a head-shrinker to a heart-specialist. I know the difference love can make for a professional psychotherapist like myself, and for a lay person like you with many friends and loved ones in deperate need of emotional help.

Every Spirit-filled Christian has access to the love of Christ, but now can we use it to heal the psychological problems we see plaguing those around us? I've called my own method for applying this divine, eternal love, the "Christian love treatment." God is the source of all authentic love, and sound psychotherapeutic techniques provide the means for effective treatment.

But you may protest, "I haven't been trained as an analyst! How can I hope to do any emotional healing?"

It's true that professional analysts like myself have certain advantages: We have spent years studying and working with the human mind and have had to be psychoanalyzed ourselves for several years in "didactic analysis." We also have a captive, highly motivated audience because people come to us with the specific objective of being healed and pay their hard-earned money for our services.

Unlike the trained therapist, you don't have either a fee or professional credentials to enhance your status in the eyes of your spouse or friend. If you see an emotional problem that you think you can help, you'll first have to establish an intimate rapport with the individual. Otherwise, your acquaintance is likely to regard you not so much as a concerned Christian friend, as a meddler.

But if you show the other person that you genuinely care and if he's willing to discuss his problem with you, there's a great deal you can do to encourage the process of inner healing. Many of the principles of psychoanalysis are easy for the Christian lay person to apply in informal, open, one-on-one conversations. We'll illustrate some of these principles in detail as we tackle specific personality problems later in this book. But first, let's take a look at six basic steps that you should follow as you allow God's Spirit to work through you to cure the emotional ills of your loved ones.

1. Find some beauty and focus on it. I don't even try to work with an individual unless I can find an element of lovableness or beauty in him. You have to be able to relate to a person to help him, and if you hate everything about him, you may do more harm than good by getting involved.

So far, I've been able to find that necessary bit of beauty in everone who has come to me for help, but at times my imagination and patience have been stretched to the breaking point. I remember one woman who came to me with a severe marital problem, and I immediately became extremely sympathetic toward her husband. She was, without doubt, the most obnoxious, hostile individual I've ever met. She snapped at me several times in the first interview, criticized my offices, and made me feel as though she had come to treat *me* for a problem, rather than the other way around. I knew I either had to discover something nice about her immediately, or get rid of her. My first reaction was to tell her to find another therapist, but I knew she had alread been to several others who had not been able to stand her abrasive manner. I was probably her last hope for help, so I decided to do my best.

After scrutinizing her face, her

personality, and her style of dress, I still hated everything I saw. Then I prayed and looked at her again, and I immediately noticed her eyes. They were the most beautiful blue eyes I had ever seen. I focused on them every time she came out with a hostile word or gesture. Her eyes were my channel through her outer barriers of hostility to the real, insecure person she was shielding underneath. As we talked, I learned she had suffered horrible experiences in a Nazi concentration camp as a child. She had been terribly hurt and was transformed from a little girl who smiled a lot to a person who pushed everyone away, including her husband, to protect herself from being hurt any more. Most of the power of her personality was directed toward keeping people at a distance, and I pointed this out in the course of therapy. After the inner healing began to take place, we were able to develop a real friendship.

At the end of her analysis, which had taken several months, she said, ''You know, you're the first person in my life who ever saw anything beautiful about me."

She had no idea that I had started with her blue eyes, and that if God had not shown them to me, I would have become just another of her discarded therapists.

2. Explore the person's family background. After establishing an initial rapport with your friend, you should spend some time listening to the story of his life. Most emotional problems we have as adults can be traced back to some traumatic experience of childhood. The parents, and especially the mother, are the keys to this step of inner healing.

From the moment you were born, you began to have experiences that indelibly shaped your personality. The way the hospital nurse picked you up, the way your mother cooed over you, the rough or loving way she put her breast in your mouth — these and thousands of other impressions were recorded on your mind and formed your personality into its essential outlines by the time you were six or seven years old. We're all capable of changing after childhood has passed, but it's much harder in adulthood than in those young, impressionable years.

There are a variety of instincts, values, and motivations that become fixed parts of our personalities in the early years. Freudian psychoanalysis has divided the human personality into three distinct centers of motivation — the id, the ego, and the superego. It can be dangerous to think of the human personality as rigidly divided or split because there are many things that we do, think, and feel that are not subject to rigid compartmentalization. But we have to have some categories, and the Freudian approach has always seemed to me to be helpful, even if it isn't perfect.

Here are a few working definitions for these three basic aspects of the personality: The *id* refers to our basic, animal instincts — the "ape" in us. Our sex drives, anger, hunger, thirst, and pleasure impulses reside here. I think the Apostle Paul was talking about his constant struggle with his own id when he said, "I cannot understand my own behaviour. I fail to carry out the things I want to do, and I find myself doing the very things I hate. . . . though the will to do what is good is in me, the performance is not, with the result that instead of doing the good things I want to do, I carry out the sinful things I do not want." (Romans 7:15, 18 - 19). A person who has no control over his id is a person who is incapable of living a responsible, civilized life.

One line of defense which our parents and other early authority figures gave us to control the id is the *superego*. The superego includes the basic values and notions of right and wrong that we accepted without question when we were youngsters: 'Johnny, you mustn't hit your sister!'' Or, ''Suzy, you have to be punished for telling that lie!''

When Catholics were told by Church authorities they could eat meat on Fridays, a friend of mine retorted, ''I don't care what the Pope says, it's wrong. Besides, what do I lose by not eating meat? I'll keep on eating fish — just in case.'' The superego, the early parental training, still controlled this person's life.

Your superego is a valuable thing because it gives you some civilizing values that help control your id. Most of us, for example, have felt like killing someone at one time or another. But something inside said, "No, it's wrong to kill," and that's often sufficient to hold the little monster inside us in check. But if we only had our superego to keep us in tow, we'd soon be in trouble. For one thing, many people have poorly developed superegos: What is reprehensible stealing to one office worker may be harmless pilfering to another employee. Or what you regard as adultery may just be healthy expression of sexuality to your neighbor. Also, the superego is highly vulnerable to rationalization or outright rejection: "Sure, my parents taught me not to steal, but I don't see any good reason for not cheating on my expense account. After all, everyone else does it. It's part of what our society expects."

It's at this point that the *ego* — your basic identity, or self, — steps in to orchestrate your personality into a harmonious whole. Your mother and father may have told you sex was a dangerous, or even a bad thing, and that training gave you a value in your superego which conflicted with your lustful id. But on your wedding night, your ego surveys the situation and concludes, "Hmm, I think we can go ahead because this is an appropriate time for a romp." The ego, in other words, employs reason to determine how and under what circumstances the id should be released. The ego also helps us evaluate the validity of the superego's rules in different circumstances.

Finally, the ego is the repository of our will. The id, or animal instincts in a man, may encourage sexual desire for another man's wife. The superego responds, "No, that's not right." The ego comes in behind the superego and says, "Not only is it not right, but I *will not* follow my sexual desires in this case." A healthy ego, in other words, helps us to evaluate our animal instincts and our culturally imposed values and make a proper decision based on good, solid reasoning.

Unfortunately, none of us has a perfect ego. Many also possess weak or excessively rigid superegos, or roaring, undisciplined ids. These psychological defects become firmly embedded during our youth, and the result is the plethora of emotional problems that plague us as adults. Let me give you an example of how malfunctions in personality development occur so that you'll have some idea about the important things to listen for as your friend is telling you his life's story.

A father complained to me that his son was not living up to his potential at school. "He's a real underachiever, that boy," the father said. "I can't figure it out because we've always told him how important hard work is for a Christian."

His wife, who was also present, had little to say, however, and she admitted to me that she had been taking tranquilizing drugs for anxiety. During an interview I had alone with the boy, I noticed he was unusually solemn and morose for a twelve-year-old.

"I've never seen you smile," I said in a lighthearted way.

"My father says Jesus never smiled," he replied. "It's sinful and wastes time to joke around — at least, that's what he told me."

That statement revealed the root of his problem: An unhappy depressed father was passing on a curse to his son. He had impressed the boy with the idea that the

114

Gospel, the ultimate truth in the universe, is not good news, but bad.

"That's not the Jesus I know," I said.

"What do you mean?"

"I think Jesus was a real joker sometimes. Remember when he changed the water into wine at the Cana wedding feast? Well, I think that showed a real sense of humor. Not only did he give them extra wine, but he made it better than the original drink so the hosts had to explain why they had saved the best wine for the end of the party."

The boy smiled slightly at that, and I knew I was making some progress.

"I can't imagine Christians not smiling," I continued. "Why, think of all the passages in the Scriptures that refer to joy, joy, joy! Make a joyful noise to the Lord . . . the wise men rejoiced exceedingly with great joy when they saw the star of Bethlehem . . . joy is one of the fruits of the Spirit that Paul writes about. How can you have joy without a big grin?"

As we discussed his background, a picture developed of a very nervous, guilt-ridden young man. His father had imposed in him an incredibly rigid value system, or superego, which gave him a negative, unrealistic approach to Christianity. He was obsessed, for example, with Christ's cross. He thought if he walked on a crack in the sidewalk which was in the shape of a cross, he would be showing disrespect to Jesus. That, at least, was his conscious interpretation of his fears and anxieties. Actually I could tell that he had a basic hostility to Christ and to God, which was rooted in a hostility to his father whom he perceived as their representative on earth. He said, "I don't want to step on anything that looks like a cross." But, translated into the language of emotions, it was clear he was *really* saying, "I'd like to stamp on *anything* that looks like a cross! The cross has made me very unhappy and caused me pain."

I pointed this out to him, and he immediately denied that was what he felt. But then I said, "You know it's not Christ and the cross you're angry at. It's your father who has made you believe Jesus — a false Jesus — is responsible for your inner pain."

He seemed to agree with that analysis, but I knew the only way to set him on the right path was to change his father's attitudes. I called the parents in for a chat and immediately got to the point. "The problem with your son is that you've taught him that he shouldn't smile," I told the father bluntly. "Your wife may be on tranquilizers, but at least she laughs once in a while. I've never seen you look happy."

He mumbled some excuse, and I could see I would have to create some healthy anxiety in him if I was going to get my point across. "You know, *you're* really the sick one," I continued. "Neither your wife nor your son is as sick as you are. You're presenting a standard your family can't adhere to."

"My mother used to rock and pray and speak in tongues when something was bothering her," he argued. "It works for her, and it works for me."

"It *doesn't* work for you!" I protested. "Look at the state your family is in! It's not working at all. Take my word for it: your son will lose his faith when he gets a little older because you're giving him a false, negative kind of religion to follow. He can't stand it, and it won't be long before he rebels and throws it over completely. His underachievement is the first step in rebelling."

The father got angry with me and left the office in a huff, but I thought I noticed a determined set to his wife's mouth as she followed him out. The son was back in to see me the next week for his regular session, and some healthy changes started to take place in the home. Gradually, the boy began showing a greater capacity for enjoying life — and faith.

After you begin thinking in terms of id, ego, and superego in dealing with your friends who have emotional disturbances, solving a problem like this will become easier for you. But I find that learning these techniques is only half the battle. Prayer and a desire to show love are even more essential because they keep you sensitive to the guidance of God's Spirit. In any case, this formation of personality characteristics during childhood and adolescence will be a recurrent theme as we move through specific emotional problems in succeeding chapters.

3. Become the Good Parent. After you've identified the problem areas in your friend's personality, you should put yourself in the shoes of the offending real parent or parents and try to guide the person toward a healthier emotional condition. This process is known as "transference" because your friend will transfer his feelings about his real parents to you and begin to relate to you as he related to his own mother and father.

You'll have to be exceptionally patient and forgiving in this stage of your relationship, because your friend will expect you to react in the same unpleasant, exploitative, or unloving way his mother or father did. When you show love, instead of hate or indifference, he'll test you, try to get you to change your behavior because it's unfamiliar to him. Most people dislike their neuroses and that's why they come looking for help. But their hang-ups are familiar and even somewhat comfortable, and the process of emotional healing can be exceptionally unpleasant and disruptive.

Part of becoming the Good Parent involves being open and honest with your friend. When I was a student analyst, I was told never to lie to a patient, and that's as true a principle as I've ever heard. People with emotional problems are often more suspicious and discerning than those who are emotionally secure. A neurotic can always see through a falsehood. If you tell a lie, and your friend perceives it or learns about it, your relationship of trust automatically goes down the drain.

One woman asked me, "You don't like me very much do you?"

Although I detested her at the time, I was tempted to say, "Sure I like you," because I don't like to make people feel bad. But I replied instead, "No, I don't like you too much right now, and here's the reason why. . . ." That bit of candor opened up new channels of communication and helped her toward a speedier solution of her problems.

To encourage this free interchange of ideas and honest feelings, I let those I'm counseling know that everything they say will be kept in strictest confidence. You should do the same with your friends and loved ones. But trust is not something you can enter into contractually. It's something you have to demonstrate on a continuing basis in your relationship.

One man said, "I guess I gotta trust you," and I replied, "You don't *gotta* do nothing. I have to earn your trust. I promise I'll never lie to you knowingly, and I also promise absolute confidence, but I expect you'll have to see it over a period of time to believe it. Whatever you say, it's between you, me, and God. If anyone talks, it will be you or God — not me!"

While there are no limits on honesty and confidentiality, there are certain limits on openness, however. There's a joke about a person who came to a therapist and said, "I've got a problem, but I don't think I can talk about it."

The therapist coaxed him to talk, and the distraught young man finally said,

"I wet the bed."

"Don't feel bad about that," the therapist said. "I wet the bed too."

That, obviously, is being too open. It's not a helpful disclosure for your friend, and, more importantly, it would just burden him with your problems when he has enough of his own. But even though there are many of my own problems I wouldn't talk about with the person I'm helping, I would never try to present myself as omnipotent, as an individual who has no problems. An honest humility and openness, tempered by discretion, gives you a vulnerability that makes it easier for other people with problems to relate to you.

4. Stress responsibility. There's a notion that contaminates much of secular psychotherapy today — the erroneous idea that we're responsible only for our own behavior. What a patient does in his life is up to him and no one else, this argument goes. Live life to the hilt and concentrate on how to maximize your own pleasure.

This approach to psychotherapy is

rooted in a hedonism that permeates our entire society. The pleasure of the moment takes precedence over a sense of duty and responsibility to others. Before I became a Christian, I conveyed this message to my patients and left out any idea of giving and helping others. By the end of this sort of analysis, I would have created a person who was completely self-centered and concerned with his own pleasures to the exclusion of any consideration for others. The patient was a sort of Frankenstein-monster, an egocentric caricature of my own unresolved problems. Everyone you try to help will inevitably become in some sense a mirror image of yourself. It's no accident that patients in therapy with Freudians have Freudian dreams, and patients with Adlerians have Adlerian dreams.

But the Christian approach to interpersonal relationships is completely different from Freudian psychotherapy. Responsibility and concern for others are keystones of our faith and are the only valid road to real self-fulfillment. We're not just individual, isolated entities, but rather are members of a variety of communities. Every patient I see and every friend you work with is a member of some group — a family, church, neighborhood, or office. The way they behave affects the kind of environment in which we all have to live.

If your friend is a Christian, you can argue convincingly that his actions affect the most important community of all — the body of Christ. A young, unmarried Christian woman came to see me because of some sexual problems she had. In a somewhat unconvincing way, she joked, "Sure, I play around a little with the guys I date, and I don't see why I shouldn't go ahead and have intercourse with them. I don't see what difference it makes to anybody but me, and I have plenty of time to do penance for my sins."

"You can joke if you like," I said. "But you know, when you do something that's wrong, you affect a lot of people besides yourself. You affect your entire family, for one thing, especially since you're still living at home. Suppose I went out and misbehaved with some women.

Every family member is involved and enmeshed with every other member. You can't harm one person without affecting everybody. The man who hurts his wife will also hurt his children — and even his cats and dogs. You often get a neurotic dog in a neurotic household. He'll either skulk around in a depressed mood or run around snapping at everyone.

"If I committed adultery, I'd hurt my entire household, and you're in a similar position. You'll hurt not only your own reputation, but that of your mother and father and brothers and sisters. Another important consideration is your church community. If you do something that you know is wrong, your actions reflect on your fellow believers. Non-Christians will have less respect for what the Church teaches. No, you're not the only one who is involved in these sexual escapades you're planning."

Psychotherapy of all types — whether on a professional's couch or in the informality of a living room — certainly should help a person realize his personal potential. But we also have to help people fit into the community. Instead of advising your friend to do something just because it means immediate pleasure and perhaps gives him more confidence in himself, you may have to say, "You should give up this pleasure because it will hurt your ability to relate to those around you."

This idea of showing responsibility in the community has solid roots in New Testament teaching. Many of the passages on loving your neighbor are accompanied by statements on the necessity of sacrificing your own wishes to help another. Perhaps the strongest passage that advocates communal responsibility is this statement of Jesus to his disciples during the Last Supper: "This is my commandment: love one another, as I loved you. A man can have no greater love than to lay down his life for his friends." (John 15:12 - 13).

As we draw closer to God and begin to love Him more intensely, the desire to assume responsibility becomes an integral part of us. Eventually, the fulfillment of our responsibilities can become effortless because of the power we get from relying completely on the Holy Spirit. This is the kind of mature spirituality which must be our goal as we work with friends whose emotional problems are preventing them from experiencing an exhilarating, totally committed walk with God.

5. Learn to handle sin and guilt. Many therapists have made the mistake of trying to remove all sense of sin and guilt from their patients. They hurt, rather than help people with this approach, because there is a valid, realistic kind of guilt, as well as a neurotic, unhealthy guilt. If you try to remove realistic guilt, you may plunge your friend into a depression because he may know he has done something wrong but will have no firm sense of morality to guide him in the proper direction.

Sometimes it's actually necessary to encourage this healthy sense of guilt and consciousness of sin. One man came in to see me about a marital problem, but I learned in our discussion that he had been inducing unintelligent, disturbed young girls to have sexual intercourse with him. I was appalled at this evil, and, knowing he was a former Catholic, I appealed to his sense of right and wrong.

"Your marital problems are related to these infidelities, but there's something else involved here," I told him. "What you're doing to those young girls is evil and sinful."

He laughed and replied, "Evil, schmevil — what does that mean? I don't believe there is any such thing as sin, or any absolute right or wrong either. I'm not into that Catholic bag any more."

"All right, if I steal your car, what do you call that?" I retorted.

"That's illegal," he said.

"Why don't we just call it gobbledegook?" I said. "In any case it's not a nice thing, is it? You say there's no evil, but what about Buchenwald? What about what the Nazis did a few years ago? What do you call that?"

He fidgeted, cleared his throat, and mumbled something about the concentration camps being "sick," but he wouldn't deny they were also evil. No intelligent person can deny it. Evil and sin do exist, and when we commit wrongful acts, we should feel guilty. In the Christian sense, sin is a transgression of the law of God. It's an act or attitude that breaks our fellowship with the Lord.

Some psychiatric scholars who denied that sin is a valid concept a few years ago have now returned to sin as a useful term. Karl Menninger, the noted psychiatrist and formerly one of the leaders in the movement against sin, acknowledged that God and the Scriptures may have been right after all. In *Whatever Became of Sin?* (Hawthorne, New York, 1973) he wrote, "a conscious sense of guilt and implicit or explicit repentance would be consequences of the revival of an acknowledgment of error, transgression, offense, and responsibility — in short, of sin."

And what would be the good of reintroducing a sense of sin in our society? "The assumption that there is sin . . . implies both a possibility and an obligation for intervention," Menninger answered. "Hence sin is the only hopeful view. The present world miasma and depression are partly the result of our self-induced conviction that since sin has ceased to be, only the neurotics need to be treated and the criminals punished. . . . As it is, vague, amorphous evil appears all around us . . . when this or that awful thing is happening . . . and yet, withal, when no one is responsible, no one is guilty, no moral questions are asked . . . we sink to despairing helplessness. . . . Therefore I say that the consequences of my proposal would not be more depression, but less. If the concept of personal responsibility and answerability for ourselves and for others were to return to common acceptance, hope would return to the world with it!''

The Apostle Paul advocated these ideas well before Menninger, so when you're working with your friend and his problems, don't be afraid to call sin what it is! But don't be judgmental as you give advice, either. You're a sinner too; except for the healing love of Christ, you'd be in the same quagmire of guilt that is disturbing the person you're counseling. You have no right to be self-righteous or to place yourself in a superior position. And if you do take a judgmental, condescending stance, you'll destroy any opportunity you may have to allow the Spirit of God to channel healing, divine love through you.

I encountered such a judgmental attitude once when I went to see a pastor about a problem with one of my children. Yes, even psychoanalysts sometimes need counseling. On the verge of tears, I said, "Pastor, this is a tremendous problem for me, and I don't know what to do. I've been praying, but for some reason, this relationship won't seem to straighten itself out."

He listened quietly and I expected we'd pray together; and he might comfort me and perhaps suggest meeting with other members of the family. But instead, when I had finished, he said roughly, "Well, you've done something wrong, Al."

"What do you mean?"

"You have to look and see if your prayer life is what it should be, and . . ."

He went on to list a half dozen other mistakes he thought I might be making, and I felt as though I had been slapped in the face. If he had just taken my hand, or

131

put a hand on my shoulder and said nothing, it would have helped a lot. Or he might have said, "Al, I know what you're going through. Fathers have to go through a lot. But let's talk about this and see how you can put more trust in the Lord."

A healing experience inside me would have started right then because I would have felt the love of Christ moving through him to me. But as it was, I sensed no warmth from him, but only disapproval and judgment. He cut off my expressions of feeling and encouraged unnecessary guilt. I knew something was wrong, and I knew the problem might be related to sin. But this pastor was insensitive about how to deal with my guilt in a way that would help me feel the presence and power of God and be able to move confidently back into a trusting relationship with Him. I finally worked my family problem out by myself, but the encounter with this pastor had taught me a valuable lesson: A counselor should never try to become the ultimate judge of sin.

6. *Introduce the meaning of life.* As I mentioned in the first part of this book, a failure to stress the meaning of life was one of the first flaws I detected in my secular psychoanalytic training and practice. A number of other psychoanalysts who were not Christians saw this deficiency, and they rallied around Victor Frankl, who founded the theory of "logotherapy," which has been called "the Third Viennese School of Psychotherapy." (Victor E. Frankl, *Man's Search for Meaning: An Introduction to Logotherapy,* Pocket Books, New York, 1959, 1963.)

Freud's theories were oriented around the idea that men are motivated by a "will to pleasure," the need to satisfy the basic animal instincts. Alfred Adler's psychology was rooted in the notion that the underlying cause of human action and emotional problems is a "will to power." Frankl, on the other hand, said that "the striving to find a meaning in one's life is the primary motivational force in man." The term "logotherapy" is taken from the Greek word *logos,* which refers to the inherently rational or meaningful structure of the universe. In stressing the importance of meaning for man, Frankl likes to quote Nietzsche, who said, "He who has a *why* to live can bear with almost any *how.*" In other words, if a peson can find an ultimate meaning to his life, he can put up with almost anything — anxiety, suffering or tragedy.

Frankl's logotherapy puts a prime emphasis on the responsibility of the individual. In order to find the meaning of life, a person must see himself as responsible to his own conscience, to society, or to God. "The majority . . . consider themselves accountable before God," he observed. "They represent those who do not interpret their own lives merely in terms of a task assigned to them but also in terms of the taskmaster who has assigned it to them." In his search for meaning man must look beyond himself and his own self-actualization, Frankl argues. He believes there are three ways in which a person can discover meaning — by achieving something, by experiencing a value such as love, or by suffering.

Frankl himself discovered meaning through suffering in Nazi concentration camps during World War II. In one of those camps, he lost a manuscript which was his life's work, and he questioned whether his life was devoid of any meaning since he didn't expect to survive. But in the pocket of a coat issued to him he found a single page torn out of a Hebrew prayer book. The paper contained the Shema Yisrael, an important Jewish prayer. "How should I have interpreted such a 'coincidence'' other than as a challenge to *live* my thoughts instead of merely putting them on paper?" he asks. Frankl found that his terrible ordeal became meaningful as he established relationships with the other inmates and helped them. His insights encouraged him to found the school of logotherapy and explore the concept of meaning in psychoanalysis after his release from the camps at the end of the war.

Frankl has influenced my own thinking because I believe the "will to meaning" that he described is actually a symptom of man's basic need to find God. Secular training can help us heal emotional wounds, such as anxiety and depression, and also physical maladies, like a deep laceration or a broken arm. But there is a deeper need, a spiritual hunger, that needs to be satisfied if a person is going to become a completely healthy human being. A commitment to Christ must saturate every part of our lives if we hope to attain this true wholeness. Man is a composite of mind, body, and soul, and we can't separate him into one or two of these parts, treat him, and expect him to get completely well. Emotional and spiritual problems are often so closely related that they should be treated together if your friend is receptive to the Gospel.

If he's not interested in spiritual matters, you should still go ahead and help him with his emotional problem, just as you would give him a bandage if he were bleeding. Remember Jesus told his disciples that in addition to preaching, they should "Cure the sick, raise the dead, cleanse the lepers, cast out devils." (Matthew 10:8). If you let your emotionally sick acquaintance know you can offer him spiritual succor and he turns you down, you've at least planted a seed for the Gospel. A few more seeds here and there by other concerned Christians may eventually prompt him to rely on Christ. It took a sackful of such seeds and a great deal of prodding by God's Spirit before I committed myself to Jesus so I know how important the cumulative spiritual effect is.

This is what the Christian love treatment is all about: Helping our friends and acquaintances with their emotional problems by showing genuine concern for them, no matter how much of our proferred help they accept or reject. The final results depend on how the Spirit of God touches a person's heart, and on how the individual responds to these divine overtures.

These six principles or steps are the framework which you should keep in mind as you consider the specific emotional problems and solutions in the following chapters. Now then, let's examine how the Christian love treatment can combat the personal hell of depression.

Chapter Five

The Valley of the Shadow of Depression

Have you ever had the feeling that life is futile . . . you don't feel like getting involved in anything . . . you don't want to get out of bed and face the inevitable gloom that seems to engulf you . . . the day is gray and unpleasant even though it's actually bright and exhilarating . . . it wouldn't really make any difference if you crashed in your car and died? Do you know anyone who has ever felt this way?

Probably both you and most of your friends have faced some of these feelings because they are the classic signs of depression, one of the three biggest emotional problems of our culture, along with boredom and anxiety. There are two common types of depression — realistic and chronic. Realistic depression results when you react to some specific mishap, like the death of a loved one. Chronic depression is more seriuos and involves an emotional sickness that has no specific immediate cause.

If your disturbed friend is a victim of a fairly constant, chronic depression, it's best to try to get him to seek out professional help. If he refuses to do this, the responsibility for helping him will land squarely on you if he asks your advice. What can you do? First of all, begin to relate to him in a way that is consistent with the six principles of the Christian love treatment that we outlined in the last chapter. Establish a trust relationship, try to isolate the earlier experiences that led to his present condition, and begin to love him as a Good Parent. Be especially sensitive to the hostility and rage that your friend may be suppressing (consciously forcing the feeling out of his mind) or repressing (unconsciously forcing the thought away). Chronic depression often results from a long-standing repressed or suppressed hostility toward one of the parents.

A young Christian man named Peter came in to see me with just such a depression. Though a talented artist, he wasn't working because he couldn't get interested enough in life to get himself moving. He was in his late twenties, but still lived at home under the influence of a dominant mother. After we had discussed his bleak attitude toward life for a few minutes, I could see that there was nothing specific he was reacting to, so I realized his problem had to stem from earlier family experiences. As he told me about his life as a youngster, a picture emerged of a mother who used a heart condition to manipulate every member of her family, including Peter. She was a woman who had to have her way and couldn't tolerate the word "no."

On one occasion, Peter had told her, "Mom, there's a great art instructor in Paris that I'd like to study under. One of my college teachers says I might be able to get a fellowship to go over there if I . . ."

But she interrupted, "Peter, you know we need you around here in case

I should get worse."

"But Mom, I . . . ."

"Peter, please, oh, Peter!" she exclaimed, and, grasping at her heart, she ran for the medicine cabinet to take some of her heart medicine.

This scenario became a regular thing in the home, with the mother keeping the other family members under her thumb through the threat of a heart attack. Peter finally just went along with her because he was afraid that if he asserted himself — if he emerged as an independent man — it would kill her.

As the rage and hostility welled up inside him, he sometimes actually admitted to himself that he hated his mother for what she was doing to him. Then he began to feel guilty and denied his hostility — just pushed it out of his mind and tried to imagine it didn't exist. His subconscious mind, in other words, had become a boiler that was on the verge of exploding because of all the pent-up rage and guilt that he had pushed back inside himself.

When he occasionally became aware of the intensity of his hatred, the strong feelings of guilt that he harbored would become almost unbearable and he would punish himself in some way. He'd go out and get drunk, and perhaps allow himself to get beat up in a bar. One time, after a heavy night of drinking, he smashed up a new car he had bought.

After listening to his story, I was finally ready to assume the role of his substitute parent, the compassionate mother he needed so desperately. "You've paid for your guilt, Peter," I said.

"No, no, there's no way I can pay for some of these feelings," he said.

"Look at what you're doing to yourself," I argued. "You've emasculated yourself by failing to go out and get a job and pursue a promising career. You rarely go out with friends for any sort of recreation. You're making no effort to meet a nice girl you could marry, and that's a shame because you're a handsome, personable fellow. When you do go out for what should be a relaxing evening, you punish yourself by getting drunk, getting hurt, smashing up a new car. Tell me, were you as depressed *after* you smashed up that car?"

He cocked his head and looked at me in a surprised way. "You know, I wasn't so depressed, and I couldn't figure it out."

"It's because you did a penance by wrecking your car and that relieved some of your guilt," I explained. "You've got to face this problem, Peter, or you're really going to hurt yourself. You're throwing your life away because your mother is manipulating you by faking a heart condition."

"But she really *does* have a heart condition!"

"Sure, but you don't believe she's having an attack every time you try to disagree with her, do you? You have to stand on your own feet and start leading an independent life. God intends for you to be your own person. It's what your *mother* is doing that's wrong and sinful, *not* your desire to be free of her influence."

"So what should I do?" he asked nervously.

"First of all, tell me what you'd like to tell your mother when she starts having

143

one of her spells and cuts you off.''

"Well, I'd like to say, ''Gee, Mom, you're putting me in a bad position, and I . . .' ''

"Come on, come on, Peter!'' I said impatiently. ''That's real hatred and burning hostility you have inside you. What do you *really* want to say? Say it, and get it all out in the open!''

"Okay, I will,'' he retorted, flushing slightly. "I'd like to tell her to drop dead! You're really a pain, Mother, because you won't let me be myself! I sometimes think I'm going to go crazy if I have to watch you grab your chest one more time. You've been making me feel guilty all my life, and sometimes I'd . . . okay, I'll say it: sometimes I really think I'd like to kill you!''

He collapsed back into his chair after this outburst, and I knew we had made the first significant step in breaking free of his mother's tyranny. In my office, he had found a forum where he could express his feelings of hostility and disagreement and not feel as though he had to keep them hidden somewhere deep inside his already troubled emotions. The Scriptures tell us not to avoid anger completely, but to express it appropriately. As Paul said in Ephesians 4:26: "Even if you are angry, you must not sin."

Peter's next step was to learn how to assert himself with his mother — not tell her he wanted to kill her, but tell her when he disagreed with her and when he was going to follow his own conscience and his own sense of God's leading, instead of allowing her to take the place of God in his life. He made some mistakes. There were a number of unnecessary arguments and harsh words that passed between him and his mother. But when she learned that running to the medicine cabinet and her other stratagems had lost their power, the way was open for a more mature mother-son relationship. Peter moved out into his own apartment, got a job, and began to develop a rather successful career as a commercial artist. He kept in touch with his parents, but in a healthier, more independent way than before.

The Spirit of God can't work effectively

in the life of a person like Peter until the depression — the emotional roadblock to his progress as a mature, committed Christian — is removed. When Peter's depression lifted, he was free to move with the Spirit and seek God's will for his life as an independent man with God-given talents that were crying to be used.

Many times you, your spouse or some friend will experience another kind of depression — one which is a reaction to some specific, recent incident that you can identify immediately. This kind of depression is often appropriate and is a signal or symptom that is telling you to take some specific countermeasure to correct the problem. For example, a sixty-five-year-old man named Carl came into my office crying and wringing his hands because he had lost his job. He was extremely depressed, and he knew exactly why.

"What use am I now?" he wailed. "I'm nothing, absolutely nothing."

His appearance made him look more like a budding bowery bum than a man who had been out of work for a month. He had a day's growth of beard and was hunched over with a drooping, sad expression on his face. His tie was hanging loose on one side of his neck and I counted at least two buttons that were missing from his shirt. Because his eyes had a slightly glassy look, I asked his wife about medication and she confirmed what I suspected: He was heavily doped-up on drugs that a physician had prescribed for his condition. He took a mood-elevator to relieve his depression during the day and had also started on depressants at night so that he could get to sleep. When I asked a question, I noticed it took him several seconds to focus in on what I was saying.

Carl had held a very important job in a big hotel as the liaison between hotel guests and airline and theater ticket sellers. He also was an expert at arranging elaborate dinners in various clubs for salesmen and visiting business executives. A change in hotel management and an over-all decline in the travel and tourist business had resulted in his job being phased out. He had no financial problems because he received a good pension and Social Security payments, but his work had been so important to him that he almost felt as though his life had ended.

"A psychiatrist we consulted suggested that we might put Carl into shock treatment — you know, to snap him out of this mood of his," explained his wife, who had insisted on attending the first session.

"Under no circumstances should you have shock treatment," I replied. "Carl is sixty-five years old, and it could really hurt him. There's often brain damage in shock treatment, and it's really a frightening experience. Sometimes, just after the experience, the patient can't even recognize people he knows."

She agreed, but I wasn't finished yet. "Also," I continued, "I want Carl to go off these pills he's taking. He's so drugged up, I don't know what his real personality is like. I have to see the real Carl if I'm going to try to help him."

"Oh, but we can't do that . . ." his wife began.

"Oh yes you can. You have to if I'm

going to work with him."

She reluctantly went along with this request, and I knew we had taken the first major step in getting Carl back into good mental health. Depression is one of the main emotional disturbances many doctors try to treat with drugs, and this reliance on pills reflects the escapist trend in our society. We want to have pleasure and avoid pain at any cost — even the cost of surrendering our own, alert personalities. One tranquilizer ad says that its product will transform snarling tigers into purring kittens, but I've found that sometimes the snarling tiger is more appropriate. Facing an emotional problem like depression squarely and learning to master it and grow out of it can be a frightening process, but you pay the price of growth if you pop a pill.

As Carl and his wife were getting up to leave, she said, "Well, we'll be back to see you this time next week, Doctor."

"I think I should work with Carl alone from now on," I said as gently as possible. "That's the only way we can expect to make real progress."

"Oh, I really think I should be here," she replied.

I looked at Carl and asked jokingly, "Say, Carl, you've over sixteen, aren't you?"

"Yeah, why?" he asked.

"You don't need your mother here, do you?" I said, still smiling, but the point got across.

She didn't like the idea, but all my sessions after that were with Carl alone. I could sense part of Carl's problem was his relationship with a strong, if not domineering wife. It was essential that she be excluded from our discussions if he was to feel free to get his feelings out in the open and master them by himself. That's something for you to keep in mind when you're working with your spouse or a friend. If you try to do any therapy while a third party is present you may find a lack of openness and honesty.

When Carl returned to my office by himself the next week, he was off the drugs, and I could see how serious his depression really was. He was a man who seemed to feel completely worthless. He constantly downgraded himself and disclosed a seriously weak ego. I knew it would be important to probe into his early background, especially his relationship with his mother, because I suspected his relationship with his wife was a continuation of his childhood experience.

Sure enough, Carl's discussion of his youth revealed a mother who was a milder version of the phony-heart-attack manipulator that Peter, in the previous illustration, had to endure. Carl's mother hadn't been quite as domineering, but her power over her son was reflected clearly by the fact that he lived with her until he was twenty-seven. She was a genuine invalid but was so afraid of being alone that she whined and complained every time he walked out of the house. She prevented him from developing any independence and made him feel like dirt. "I hope you won't get married until I'm gone," she told him. "I think a son who doesn't watch out for his own family is not worth a nickel."

Carl had become so fed up with this treatment that he decided he had to take a day off and go out with some friends. When he returned, his mother was dead. He had been plagued by guilt feelings ever since, and he married a woman who in many respects provided a mother substitute for him. She was as manipulative as the mother and tried to run Carl's life by stressing that he was not really quite as good as other people. The result was that Carl's feelings of worthlessness were reinforced. His ego, or sense of personal identity and value as a human being, remained weak. Subconsciously, he had married his wife in the hope of re-creating the situation with his mother and resolving it. But instead, he just opened up the old mother-son wounds and sank deeper into the quicksand of a poor self-image.

As a final line of defense, Carl became a workaholic and devoted his entire life to his company, but even in this environment he couldn't escape the influence of his wife and mother. He worked all his life for the same hotel, and projected into the occupational authority figures, the business executives around him, his feelings toward the women who dominated him. Like his mother and his wife, these superiors also downgraded, manipulated, and exploited him: "We can't give you a raise this year, Carl. You're lucky we're keeping you on at all because you'd have trouble finding a job any place else."

My work was cut out for me. I had to become the Good Parent for Carl and take over as the dominant person in his life for a while. That meant overcoming the influence of his strong-willed wife, and I knew it wouldn't be easy. I believed Carl was a much more competent person than either his former employers or his wife had allowed, and I watched for an opportunity to point this fact out to him. By building him up, I would help strengthen his damaged ego and start the healing process.

My opportunity came during our third session, when I got a call from my cousin Rudy, about a convention in San Antonio we were planning to attend. He asked if I'd checked the plane reservations, and I replied, "No, I haven't had a chance to call the airport yet. I don't even know what airlines fly down there."

Carl, who was sitting across from me during this conversation, interrupted in an authoritative voice, "Braniff, flight . . ." He rattled off the days and times, and told me who to call and what to ask. I sat there with my jaw sagging.

When I hung up the phone, I said, "Carl, you've just shown me something important about your abilities. You're a very valuable person, and I think you owe it to yourself to go back to work."

"What kind of work? Who would have me? I'm sixty-five years old!"

"It's not a question of who would have you, but whether they can afford to pay for your expertise," I said. "You shouldn't just take any job. You have knowledge and personal contacts that would give any company an advantage."

We began to go over his job qualifications, and I saw he had other talents I hadn't been aware of at first. He had some bookkeeping experience and had managed a small staff at the hotel. As we talked about what course of action he should take, I could see a new confidence surge into him. His wife had always belittled him. His company, in a surrogate mother role, had kept him in a constant state of anxiety about his job and undercut any tendency he had to develop self-confidence. He was so afraid of rejection that he had stayed on at the same company for nearly forty years, rather than test his abilities on the open marketplace.

When Carl finally decided to look for a job, I knew I was about to face the ultimate challenge to my authority. He had transferred his feelings about his mother and wife to me, and I was helping him to heal myself, but he had to have a final victory over his wife's influence. I called her in and got to the point immediately: "Carl has to go back to work," I declared.

"He's in no condition to work!" she protested.

It was obvious she preferred to keep him on medication so that he would cause no trouble with his depression. She felt comfortable having him deteriorate around the house as she collected his pension and Social Security checks. I could see that I would have to do some therapy on her by scaring her and creating a little constructive guilt.

"If he goes along this way, he's going to get much worse," I said. "If he goes out and gets a job and starts feeling important, he'll be around another ten years. But at the rate he's going now, he'll be dead within the year." At this point, I looked directly at her. "And if that happens — if you take the easy way out with these drugs and keep him around the house — you'll have to hold yourself *directly responsible* for his death. You'll be the only one who's guilty."

She shifted uncomfortably in her chair and soon agreed with my advice. Carl went out and got a part-time job with a bank, where he worked for about six hours a week setting up travel schedules for executives. He visited me a few weeks later, and I hardly recognized him. Wearing a spiffy sports jacket and stylish slacks, he looked like a new man. All he had needed to escape his depression was someone who would encourage him to overcome his wife's resistance and get another job.

Sometimes, though, the remedy for a serious depression may involve even more extensive work with the "healthy" spouse than I did with Carl's wife. If your husband or wife is depressed, you should take a good look at yourself — *you* may be the main cause of the emotional problem. Let me explain by introducing you to Ellen, a Christian woman in her late thirties who came to me with a severe depression. Her husband, Michael, had been an alcoholic, and she had maintained a cheerful, positive frame of mind when he was harassing her and the rest of the family with booze. But about four years before I met her, her husband had undergone a radical conversion to Christianity and had immediately conquered his drinking problem. Ellen began suffering from severe depressions at the same time and they continued until she decided to come to me for help four years later.

"I'm sometimes afraid I'm going to kill myself," she said. "I've had shock treatments, been under medication, but nothing seems to help. I'm always on the verge of tears."

"How about your husband?" I asked. "Is he still all right?"

"Oh yes. Michael's so good and great. He keeps getting more and more involved in Christian work. I've tried to be as committed as he is, but it doesn't seem to work for me. I've had several deliverances from demons, but that hasn't helped. I'm basically not a very good person, I guess. I just don't know where I'm going — nothing seems to be worthwhile in my life."

As we discussed her family background, I learned that both her parents had been alcoholics, and they didn't pay much attention to her. They were always fighting with one another or were in such a stupor they couldn't communicate with their kids. Ellen didn't ask herself, "My mother gets drunk — what's wrong with her?" Instead, like most children, she vested her parents with omnipotence and decided nothing could be wrong with them, so something had to be wrong with her. Her question as a little girl became,

"My mother doesn't love me — what's wrong with *me?*"

When a child like Ellen doesn't feel loved, she doesn't feel worthwhile as a person, either, and this low view of herself stayed with her up into adulthood. In an attempt to heal the deep emotional wounds, she tried to re-create her childhood traumas by marrying a man who had a drinking problem, just like her parents. She had learned to put up with Michael's shenanigans and began to find value in her life by being the long-suffering wife. She felt she was helping him and in an unconscious way she was repairing her relationship with her drunken parents. But when Michael accepted Jesus and overcame his alcoholism without any help from Ellen, she felt useless, and depression swept over her. The failure of Ellen and many others to escape the emotional problems imposed on them by the mistakes and spiritual disobedience of their parents reminds me of an Old Testament passage that's part of the Ten Commandments: ". . . For I, Yahweh your God, am a jealous God and I punish the father's fault in the sons, the grandsons, and the great-grandsons of those who hate me." (Exodus 20:5).

Wives of reformed alcoholics are sometimes harder to help than the alcoholic himself. When the drunk starts to dry out, the wife may resist his cure because she fears that the main purpose in her life — putting up with a lousy husband — will disappear. I don't know how often I've seen wives of alcoholics begin to complain about their husbands' therapy sessions as the husband starts to show improvement: "You're going to therapy twice a week, and you should be doing the gardening!" one wife told a patient of mine. "We can't afford the money you're putting out for treatment. The kids need music lessons, I need a new dress. . . ."

After his cure, if the husband is self-righteous and impressed with his own virtue, as Michael was, the wife's loss of purpose and meaning can be compounded. I asked Michael to come in for a talk and found him to be a person who was outwardly serene, but only because he refused to listen to things he found unpleasant to hear. He was completely oblivious to the feelings and sensitivities of others, including his wife. After we had talked for a few minutes, I wanted to make a point from the Bible because I knew he was an evangelical Christian and would recognize the Scriptures as authoritative.

But as soon as I opened the book, he demanded, "What Bible are you using?"

"The Jerusalem Bible," I replied.

"What kind of a Bible is that?" he said with a slightly condescending sneer.

"It's a scholar's Bible," I shot back. "I wouldn't expect you to be familiar with it."

I immediately knew that was a nasty thing to say and realized that I had fallen into a trap that at one time or another catches all therapists and will stymie you, too, if you're not careful. In psychoanalytic terms, the mistake I made is called "countertransference." In trying to counsel him and get him to transfer his feelings toward his wife to me, I had inadvertently gotten too emotionally involved myself. I had transferred my own innate, hostile feelings about self-righteous people like Michael back toward him, rather than holding my own emotions in check.

Finally, I said, "Look, I'm sorry I reacted to you that way. You hit me, and I hit you back, and that wasn't right. But I'm very angry with you — I want you to know that. Can I be honest with you? If I can, I think it may reveal something about your relationship with your wife."

"Sure, go ahead," he replied. He honestly didn't know that he had done anything wrong and was interested in improving himself and becoming a more effective Christian.

"You come on as a nasty, sarcastic kind of guy," I said. "You come in here as a Christian, but you provoke very un-Christian feelings in me toward you. I can always bring in another Bible to read from if you like. But that's not the problem. Your problem is your hostility, and I don't think you even know you *are* hostile."

He admitted that he didn't, and I could

see he was genuinely concerned about his own spiritual growth. It was hard for me to be so honest with him because I like to sit in my chair and tell people what wonderful attributes they have. But that's not what Michael needed. He needed honest criticism about his personality if his relationship with Ellen was to be repaired.

"Ellen can't be as open with you as I can because you don't give her any opportunity to express the resentment and frustration she feels toward you," I said. "You appear to be self-righteous, and she knows you are. But she can't communicate how you irritate her, so she gives up. Her depression is the result. She's turning her hostility back into herself because you won't allow her any means to express it. You cut her off with a counterfeit kind of forgiveness and moral superiority. Do you understand what I'm saying?"

"I think so," he replied. "But what can I do?"

"Okay, I'm going to encourage Ellen to express her hostilities toward you and toward her mother, and I want you to respond — get angry at her if you feel like it. But at least listen to her — don't cut her off.''

With some hesitation Michael agreed, though he objected at first because he felt it was un-Christian to show anger. I explained, however, that Jesus vented anger on a number of occasions — even toward members of his family. When his mother, Mary, informed Jesus about the lack of wine at the marriage feast at Cana, he responded with apparent irritation: ''Woman, why turn to me? My hour has not come yet.'' (John 2:4). He also expressed his displeasure with the moneychangers in the Temple by using physical violence. (Matthew 21:12). And he railed against the religious hypocrites of his day in rather raw language: ''Alas for you, scribes and Pharisees, you hypocrites! You who are like whitewashed tombs that look handsome on the outside, but inside are full of dead men's bones and every kind of corruption.'' (Matthew 23:27).

When Jesus and Paul advised against anger (see Matthew 5:22 and Ephesians 4:26 - 27), they were clearly referring to unjustified anger or grudges, rather than a healthy ventilation of feelings to clear the air. Justifiable anger is the method we use to release pentup, repressed hostilities to begin the journey toward emotional recovery. At my suggestion, Ellen began to show this kind of anger when she felt Michael was being too overbearing. The couple seemed to be handling their problems rather well until Michael called me one day and cried, ''This anger business is fine, but now she's getting worse!''

''What are you talking about?'' I asked.

''She won't go to church with me now,'' he said. ''I insisted she go to church with me this Sunday, and she put her foot down and said she wouldn't.''

''Did she say why?'' I asked.

''Yes. She said she hadn't been getting anything out of church lately because she thought I was trying to tell her what to believe, and she says she wants to take some time off and think things through.''

''That may be the best thing that could happen to her, spiritually speaking,'' I replied. ''She's had a strong connection with the church. Her friends are there; her social life centers in Christian activities. Think about this thing rationally, Michael. You know she'll eventually go back to church. Just give her a little freedom. Let her vent her anger, and she'll be a much better wife in the long run.''

He reluctantly agreed, and, as I had predicted, Ellen was back in church again the following week. In a way, I think her approach to worship may have been quite valid scripturally because she and Michael were having a misunderstanding and she felt she had to resolve it before she could worship properly. This attitude is in line with what Jesus advised in the Sermon on the Mount: ''. . . if you are bringing your offering to the altar and there remember that your brother has something against you, leave your offering there before the altar, go and be reconciled with your brother first, and then come back and present your offering.'' (Matthew 5:23 - 24).

Ellen's depression lifted as she began to express her feelings. She was well on the road to a complete healing of her personality because she now had a sensitive

Christian husband who was willing to help her. She manifested her hostility indiscriminately at first, like a child who has discovered the devastating power of saying "no." Ironically the child often says no to candy as well as to pabulum, and Ellen also showed more anger at times than was necessary. But she learned, just as the child learns, and now she and her husband have settled into a mature, Christian marriage.

As I sat in on a prayer meeting one evening I heard a priest say, "In a true Christian community, there is no anger." This priest, to put it bluntly, didn't know what he was talking about. The biggest problem that threatens any community, Christian or otherwise, is unresolved hostility that leads to depression and misunderstanding. If I don't resolve the occasional feelings of hostility that I feel toward my wife as I sit across the breakfast table from her, I may end up disliking her. That priest was sowing the seeds for depression everywhere he spoke because he was encouraging the suppression and repression of anger and hostility. Real

Christian love doesn't mean ignoring or running away from unpleasant feelings. The love of Christ, which can cure depression, involves understanding the problem of your friend or spouse, helping to resolve it, and and finally, forgiving any excesses as the healing begins to close the inner wound.

Sometimes, in trying to help your friend overcome his depression, you may trace the roots of his difficulty back to a sense of meaninglessness in life, a feeling that daily existence has lost its zest. This half-dead, hollow attitude stems from our second major emotional ill, which most of us know quite well as boredom.

Chapter Six

The Battle
Against Boredom

Boredom is an emotional by-product of a technological society which we haven't learned to control. The meaning of our routine, paper-pushing work escapes us, and feelings of lethargy and sluggishness may make each step seem an unbearable physical labor. Indifference takes over when the victim of boredom finally sits down at his office desk or gets around to pulling out the vacuum cleaner to do the floors.

If your spouse or some friend suffers from this pervasive mental sickness, which often results in depression, you can take heart because there's an effective antidote. First of all, try to isolate the cause of the boredom. Usually, you can trace the problem back to one of two sources — a lack of meaning in life, or a pent-up hostility than can find no other release. Let's examine each of these types of boredom and see how the Christian love treatment can provide a remedy.

Boredom that results from a lack of meaning in life and in work can bother Christians as well as non-Christians. Even believers have allowed themselves to be seduced away from a total, unwavering commitment to Christ by the tempations of our society. An inner filling with the Spirit of God is the only sure strategy in the battle against boredom, and the only way to a sense of vocation and purpose. But believers as well as nonbelievers have succumbed to the sirens of Hollywood and Madison Avenue advertising. Instead of being focused on Christ, we become addicted to tranquilizers, liquor, and the most subtle substitute of all — television.

The heroes and heroines of the movie and television screens have access to all the attractive material things of life — nice homes and apartments, sleek cars, unlimited expense accounts for travel.

Many of them seem to partake of every imaginable pleasure, including a surfeit of sex, never-ending vacations, and jobs that provide a springboard to fantastic adventure. Christians who see this gaudy, unrealistic scene may be enticed into these thought patterns by thinking. "These people are leading more exciting lives than I am. It would be fun to watch them a little more closely." It's only a short step from this attitude to the idea that it's more meaningful to live *through* the lives of these fantasy figures than develop a sense of purpose and direction in our own less glamorous daily existence.

The advertising copy that bombards us every day reinforces this hedonistic value structure. Even if our defenses are strong, we may give in and start accumulating the items that the movie stars, advertisers, and salesmen tell us we need to be happy and satisfied. We rely more and more on our television sets to guide the course of our lives and help us escape the real world, which looks increasingly boring in comparison to the exotic scenes on the tube. That first favorite program becomes a second and a third, until finally, we're hooked.

We can become so addicted to the television set that it becomes an idol that impedes communications with other members of the family and with God. I know what I'm talking about because I was a TV addict at one point. Although I had accepted Christ, material things meant a great deal more to me then than they do now. I hadn't integrated Christ completely into my work: I was a "closet Christian," as I told you in a previous chapter, and I hadn't experienced the exhilaration of a working life completely controlled by the Spirit of God. The chair in front of my television set was the *sanctum sanctorum,* the holy of holies, that enabled into me to escape boredom, to live in a fantasy world with people and places that were far beyond what my time, money, or opportunities would allow.

One evening, though, when I came home from work and was looking forward to some of my favorite programs, my wife said, "Al, the TV set broke today."

I was furious. "The children broke it,

didn't they?" I retorted heatedly. "They haven't learned how to take care of things. You give them something, and they tear it apart. They don't know the meaning of money. That set was fine when we bought it."

Florence let me blow my steam, and then she replied quietly, "Al, do you realize that set is ten years old?"

I couldn't believe it. I *wouldn't* believe it at first, but as I thought back over the years, I knew she was right. I had actually been sitting in front of that set, glued to a flickering screen, ignoring my family for hours on end — every evening for ten straight years. I spent some time examining my conscience that night, and I didn't like what I saw. My actions showed that things — material, lifeless things — had become more important to me than people. I was concerned about whether my television was operational, and I should have been concerned about whether my kids were operational.

My eye wandered over several favorite scriptural passages and finally focused on Isaiah 44. I read the section beginning with verse 9: ". . . all makers of idols . . . are nothing and the works they prize are useless. . . . The blacksmith works it over the fire and beats it into shape with a hammer. . . . The wood carver takes his measurements, outlines the image with chalk, carves it with chisels, following the outline with dividers. He shapes it to human proportions, and gives it a human face . . . he makes an idol of it and bows down before it. Half of it he burns in the fire . . . with the rest of it he makes his god, his idol; and falls down before it and worships it and prays to it. 'Save me,' he says 'because you are my god.' . . . They never think, they lack the knowledge and wit to say . . . 'Am I to bow down before a block of wood?''

I saw everything too clearly now. That block of wood was a television set, an idol which I had raised up to deliver myself from boredom and dissatisfaction. It was an ironic and shameful state of affairs for me of all people, because I had access to the God of the universe who had promised to satisfy all my needs. I remembered how important a scratch on my car had seemed. A lost garden tool. I had spent precious years unconsciously getting enmeshed in a false value system that had been subtly undermining my family and work relationships.

I immediately repented of the television addiction I had allowed to erode my life and opened myself up to the leading of God's Spirit. To my surprise, I found that God could turn my wasted years of television to His purposes as people with similar problems came to me for help. One such person was Ethel, who was married to Harry, a bank clerk. She told me she was running into marital difficulties and was afraid the result would be a divorce.

"Harry's too detached, for some reason," she said. "I don't feel close to him. He doesn't seem interested in me or the children. In fact, raising the kids is a one-person job — mine."

I told her to ask Harry to come in to see me, but he resisted at first. When he finally made an appointment, it was obvious that he thought everything at home was fine. But our job as therapists is to afflict the comfortable, as well as comfort the afflicted. I could see that his sense of comfort was illusory because the other members of his family weren't happy, so I determined to get to the bottom of the problem. As Alfred Adler put it, I "spit in his soup," or began to probe through his comfortable psychological veneer to see what lay underneath.

The image that finally emerged was one of a profoundly bored man. He was a bank clerk who had a routine kind of job. He could see no meaning in it, so he tried to find some pleasure, some escape when he arrived at home in the evenings, by gravitating toward the TV tube. He became a football addict and would spend all day on two of the most important family days of the year — Thanksgiving and New Year's Day — in front of the screen.

"I can't even talk to you!" Ethel screamed at him one day, but Harry just grunted noncommittally and reached over for another can of beer. He always had a steadily dwindling six-pack at his side, and almost seemed like an extension of the beer ads which he watched almost as avidly as he did the main programs: Schaefer is the one beer to have, when you're having more than one. . . ." went the jingle. Harry tapped his fingers in time with the music and had many more than one.

It was a great escape, and Harry's life became an unreal fantasy as he merged with the television set. His job, in contrast to the excitement and adventure he saw on TV, became even more boring, and his family relationships fell into neglect. Boredom had driven him to an unsatisfactory television-and-beer substitute for authentic meaning in his life.

I noticed Harry had a sense of humor, so I used jokes to make my points with him. "How's your wife?" I asked when he came in for our second session.

He gave me a questioning look and said, "Well, she's okay, I guess. She took the kids to the park this afternoon."

"No, no, not *that* wife," I replied. "I'm talking about Zenith."

He laughed, and immediately became more comfortable with me. We both knew that television addiction was one of his biggest problems, and it was best to get the issue out in the open.

"What I can't understand, what's so painful about life that you have to waste your abilities and energies?" I said. "You're a warm, nice guy, and you have a lot to offer in relationships. Why do you head for these sterile gratifications, like drinking and television? You're like the man who Jesus said took his money and, instead of investing it wisely, buried it. You have potential but you're sitting on it, not using it. What's so unpleasant about life?"

Harry said his job was uninteresting and the only real joy he got out of life was to escape into television programs and reinforce this pleasure with a few six-packs. Since it was evident that his main problem was a lack of meaning, I began to probe his religious views and his over-all orientation toward what was valuable in life. He was a nominal Christian who at least gave lip service to the Lordship of

Christ, and I found I was able to point him rather easily toward Christianity in his search for meaning.

"You know, Jesus said it's better to give than to receive," I said. "But you keep taking in. You're completely into yourself, completely self-centered. You're like a big sponge, sucking in the nonsense on the television screen, downing those beers, and what do you have to show for it when you go to bed on Saturday night? What do you have after twelve hours of television?"

"Nothing much," he admitted.

"Right! You have six empty beer cans, a blank TV set, and a blank mind as well. Your children aren't relating to you, your wife doesn't feel beautiful any more." I hesitated for a moment to let this sink in and then continued. "Some other guy may find her beautiful one of these days. You have to face the fact that your marriage is hurting. You're vulnerable."

"So what should I do?" he asked.

"First of all, let's get your job straightened out. What do you think you can do to relieve this sense of boredom you feel? That's at the root of your problems, you know."

"Leave? Find another job?"

"Do you really think that would solve anything? Where would you go?"

He thought for a moment and shook his head. "You're right. I'd just end up in another bank job. It would be the same."

"What do you think God would want you to do?" I asked. "If you decide to commit your vocational life to Him completely, what do you think you should do?"

He shrugged. "All I can think of is the people I work with. Jesus always said to love others. There's certainly nothing in the work itself that's especially interesting."

As far as I was concerned, he had hit the nail on the head. In most jobs, including my own, the only thing that makes the work worthwhile is the human relationships you develop, the fellowship and opportunities to help and be helped, advise and be advised. The human element, the opportunity to show love, is what makes most jobs interesting and meaningful. When a solid personal relationship is established, it's possible for co-workers to get involved in deeper conversations about the meaning of work and life and about the claims of Jesus Christ.

Harry is still in his same job now, several months after our initial meeting, but his attitude has been totally transformed. He actually regards his job as a challenge to witness about his faith, both in his words and his deeds. He's also moved toward a greater involvement with his wife and kids, and spends more time with them and practically no time in front of his television set. Because of Harry's openness to the Spirit, the only real source of meaning, Jesus Christ, has been substituted for the hollow blaring of a television set and the rattling of beer cans.

Harry's problem — a lack of a sense of vocation and meaning in his work — is something that plagues most of us at one time or another. Nobody is immune, not even full-time religious workers. I was asked to speak to a group of nuns who had complained of boredom, depression, and some dissension in the house where they lived. I observed them for a while and asked a few questions before I stood up to give my talk. Then I said, "From what you've told me and from what I've seen, you need a sense of vocation. You've lost your way and become irrelevant to the community around you. That's why you're running into these emotional problems."

I wasn't sure what to expect after such a critical start. Sisters can be funny sometimes, and I half-expected one of them to say, "How dare this upstart!" and stamp out of the room. But they listened attentively, so I continued: "Some of you may think you're too old to change your ways, but remember Abraham and Sarah. They were older than any of you when God used them. Your real vocation may be just beginning. The outside community hasn't been feeling your presence as disciples of Jesus Christ because you've been sitting in front of the boob tube here when you should be out evangelizing." I pointed to the television set which had been on until I got ready to give my speech. My talk continued for about two hours, and when I had finished, one of the women said, "Why don't you go on and talk for another hour? I think this is just what we need to hear."

The next day, one of them called me and said, "You know, eight of those nuns you talked to were partially deaf, but they heard everything you said. They can't even hear the TV when it's on, but they heard you. And they're already started planning how they're going to influence the community."

Boredom vanished in that convent, and with the help of Christ it can disappear from the life of any person whose basic problem is a lack of a sense of vocation. One of my earliest encounters with the concept of vocation involved an encounter I had as a kid in Brooklyn with an Irish laborer who lived near us. He was often dirty from his labors, but my mother stressed that this was "clean dirt" because he had earned his wages honestly. Unlike many of the other workers I saw who came home half-bombed or irritable, Mr. Riley walked over to me with a big smile on his face and said, "Alphonse, who is the most important person in the world?"

"Pope Pius?" I wondered.

"No, you're wrong. Try again."

"President Roosevelt?"

"No, wrong again."

"Mayor La Guardia?"

"Nope."

"I give up — who is it?" I said.

"You are," he replied, "because Jesus died on the cross to save you."

In this way Mr. Riley even witnessed about his faith when he was commuting, and his cheerful manner showed his life had been profoundly affected by his faith. I believe that's what vocation, or a sense of purpose and direction in the primary tasks of our life, means. If we assume that God has put us in a certain job or position or location because He needs us there, then we'll focus on letting the light of Christ shine through us to our fellow workers. Most boredom, which stems from a lack of meaning, cannot survive in such an atmosphere of love.

The second kind of boredom results

from repressed or suppressed hostilities. The outward signs of listlessness and indifference are similar, but this other boredom requires a different kind of treatment.

Tom, a top sales executive for a large wholesale machinery company came in to see me one afternoon in a state of near panic. He had been on a serious drinking binge the night before, and the police had picked him up in an alley and taken him home. He was unhurt, but the experience had shaken him up so much he decided he needed help.

"I'm afraid I'm on the verge of alcoholism," he told me.

"Why do you think you drink so much?" I asked.

He smiled grimly. "I know exactly why. It's because of my job. It bores me to death, but I can't afford to quit because I'm paid too well and I don't know where else to go."

"So you drink to escape from the boredom?"

"No doubt about it," he said candidly. "And the problem has been getting worse during the past year. I don't know what to do about it."

As he described his job, it seemed interesting enough on the surface. He dealt with a variety of people, had a significant amount of managerial control, and made a lot of money. But then the real source of his problem surfaced.

"Actually, I really hate my job because of the lousy things I'm expected to do," he admitted, his eyes lowered.

"Like what?" I probed.

"Well, these buyers come in from out of town, and I'm expected to impress them — you know, wine and dine them. And they expect to be set up with women."

"And you find the girls for them?"

"Right. I feel like a pimp. I've developed a catalogue of women over the years — pictures, ages, dimensions, the kinds of sexual services they provide. Here, I'll show you." He pulled out a weathered notebook which was filled with snapshots of women and scribblings about their characteristics.

"It's sort of like a horse show, a

186

stable," I remarked, looking at the book.

"Right, and I'm sick of it. I hate to go to work in the morning. I sit at my desk and feel like I'm going to sleep. It's so boring."

"It's not just that you're bored," I said. "You're also very angry at the business and at your superiors for expecting you to perform this way. This anger and hostility is the cause of your feelings of boredom, so what we have to do is figure out how to get rid of your hostilities."

In our discussions, Tom indicated that he had been brought up as a Catholic and still attended Mass. His mother and father were extremely authoritarian, and his experience with priests and nuns reinforced the idea that you always said "yes" to authority figures. You didn't question them. Also, his parents had impressed him with the idea that if you wore expensive suits and had big cars, you were a success. Success was measured only in terms of material things and income levels.

Because his parents could not tolerate disobedience, they rewarded passivity on his part. His Church, with its, "yes, Sister" system, also discouraged independent thought. If he went along and gave all the right answers from his little catechism, he was patted on the head. If he questioned anything or gave an unusual answer, he was punished. These experiences made him angry, but he had no means to express his frustration. The cumulative, unreleased hostility toward all authority — including his employers — had intensified over the years and now was manifesting itself in his boredom and incipient alcoholism.

His religious background made him quite sensitive to the inconsistency between the values he espoused at work and the values he gave lip service to at church. Unlike many people in our society, he felt uncomfortable rationalizing away his inconsistencies. He wanted to live a Christian life, but he was afraid to relinquish the security he had with his job. I knew that in my pre-Christian practice I would have said, "You're just creating unnecessary anxieties for yourself. This is part of the society in which we live. You can't beat it, so join it. These girls you deal with are selling themselves, and it's part of the game we all have to play." I would have tried to eliminate his feeling of guilt then, but as Tom sat in front of me, I realized the best approach was to *use* his guilt feelings to get him to change.

"You're right to feel bad and inconsistent about what you're doing," I said. "You're quite justified in feeling guilty because it's not what Christ would want you to do. But the question now is what can you do about it?"

At this point I assumed the role of his Good Parent and became much less authoritarian, though hopefully more authoritative, then his real parents. "You know, it's all right to feel anger and rebel against a system that you think is perpetrating a wrong," I said. "It's your duty to vent your hostility and just quit the job sometimes. You may feel insecure at first, but in the long run it's the only way to save yourself as a human being."

Throughout this discussion — especially when he opened up to me about his dealings with call girls — I suppressed my own inclination to say, "That's wrong and sinful!" I may have felt that, but saying it would have driven Tom directly out of my office. It can be disastrous in a counseling situation like this to be judgmental at the outset and start telling a person that his acts are evil and he must stop what he's doing or face the wrath of God. Also I avoided any appearance of being shocked by his revelations. That might have made him think I was rejecting him as a person and he would have lost his sense of openness with me. Bartenders are popular for this very reason: They just listen to people without condemning, without judging. Who knows? If Jesus had said, ''Do not judge, and you will not be judged,'' (Matthew 7:1) in our own day, He might even have cited bartenders as a good example of His teaching.

Sometimes, establishing a nonjudgmental, listening relationship may be all that's necessary to effect emotional healing in your own spouse or friend. If a person feels free to let all his hostility and pain spew forth, this ventilation will bring about an inner catharsis that can work wonders. Sin is painful when it's held inside and nothing is done about it, but if your friend feels free to get his mistakes and deficiencies out into the open, your relationship with him will be strengthened. He'll feel closer to you and sense he can talk about his mistakes, learn from you and have his heart and mind healed through a bond of love.

In my relationship with Tom, just such a love bond developed because I never condescended to him. He recognized on his own that his actions were against the will of God. And I felt free to advise him about courses of action I believed were essential for his mental health: "If you continue to drink," I said, "they'll take your body home for good one of these days."

I also began to use Scripture in my conversations with him because I knew he recognized the Bible as significant spiritual authority. "You know, you look at these prostitutes just as broads who sell themselves, but in reality they're disturbed young women who can't get into a relationship with a man. Most of them have the emotions of children. Do you suppose any of them ever had any

Christian training?"

He shifted uncomfortably, "I don't know. I suppose a lot of them did, but obviously they didn't take it very seriously."

"I imagine they were exposed to Chrisitanity," I replied. "Some of them probably bleieved in Jesus once, and that reminds me of this verse from Matthew 18:6. Let me read it to you: '. . . anyone who is an obstacle to bring down one of these little ones who have faith in me would be better drowned in the depths of the sea with a great millstone around his neck.' That's what's bothering you, Tom," I said. "You can fool your conscious mind, but not your subconcious. Your conscience is begging you to stop what you're doing with these poor women."

Tom realized that the best solution to his drinking and boredom, as well as to the anger and frustration that lay underneath, was to get out of his job and try something else. His employers and co-workers thought he was crazy when he turned in his resignation and they tried to

192

talk him out of it, but his mind was made up. He knew he might have to give up his big house with its swimming pool and move into a smaller place until he could get set up somewhere else. But he realized he had no choice if he wanted to put his life back on an even keel. He eventually set up his own business and found a greater peace with himself and with God.

The more routine a person's life is, the more likely it is that he'll experience some degree of boredom. But if boredom becomes a way of life for someone you know, as it did for Harry and Tom, you should immediately start working on the problem because soon every aspect of his life will be infected with the desire to escape. Alcoholism, pill-popping, and television addiction are often symptoms which can be traced back to boredom. And the boredom itself will probably be rooted either in some pent-up hostility or in a lack of ultimate meaning in life — a failure to live a life of commitment to Christ.

Chapter Seven

Have No Anxiety

Several years ago, someone told me a story about a man with a wife who woke him up every night for twenty straight years. She would cry, "Oh, John, there's a burglar downstairs! I can hear him walking around!"

And each night, John rolled wearily out of bed and plodded down to the living room, only to find that the real problem was his wife's imagination. Finally, at the end of the second decade of their marriage, he went through his nightly routine with her, but this time, he saw a masked man rummaging through their silverware.

"Thank goodness!" he shouted to the surprised burglar. "Come on upstairs! I want you to meet my wife — you'd never believe how long she's been expecting you!"

I've told this story to people who are suffering from anxiety, and the humor sometimes helps them get a perspective on their own problem. But anxiety is usually no laughing matter for the millions of people who suffer from it. Along with depression and boredom, I regard it as one of the three main emotional disturbances we confront in our society. Christians as well as non-Christians encounter this problem, even though a peaceful, anxiety-free mental state is one of the benefits a committed Christian life holds for us.

The Apostle Paul wrote, "There is no need to worry; but if there is anything you need, pray for it, asking God for it with prayer and thanksgiving, and that peace of God, which is so much greater than we can understand, will guard your hearts and your thoughts, in Christ Jesus." (Philippians 4:6 - 7). Paul's advice echoes the extensive teaching of Jesus about anxiety in the Sermon on the Mount: "That is why I am telling you not to

195

worry about your life and what you are to eat, nor about your body and how you are to clothe it. Surely life means more than food, and the body more than clothing! ...Set your hearts on his kingdom first, and on his righteousness, and all these other things will be given you as well. So do not worry about tomorrow: tomorrow will take care of itself. Each day has enough trouble of its own.'' (Matthew 6:25, 33 - 34).

How few Christians live lives that conform to this calm, inner peace and trust that Christ described! Yet there is a consistent promise throughout the New Testament that we can get rid of our anxieties. What are the factors that prevent us from attaining this relaxed state of mind?

There are two basic kinds of anxiety that you or your acquaintances may experience. The most straightforward type, called "realistic" or "acute" anxiety, is triggered by some concrete, easily identifiable incident in your life. If the economy is in bad shape and everyone in your firm is losing his job, then you have good cause to be anxious or worried about your own occupational fatge.

The second kind of anxiety, which is designated as "free-floating" or "chronic," may result from your childhood experiences and cause you to worry about things that, objectively speaking, a reasonable person shouldn't be concerned about. In other words, if the economy is doing well, no one has been fired from your company in years and your superiors have been praising your work, you have no reason to worry about losing your job. If you feel insecure under these circumstances, you're probably suffering from free-floating anxiety.

Unlike depression and boredom, which often ends in depression, anxiety is characterized by a sense of being agitated and frustrated, and a tendency to run in circles without getting much accomplished. The anxious person, far from being lethargic or uninterested in things, is overly concerned about the possibilities of his environment. But his mental and physical activity are often unproductive because he lives in a constant state of fear.

Now let's examine some of the ways that an application of Christian love can help a person overcome realistic or acute anxiety. A former Foreign Service worker named Ray, a Christian who was in his fifties, came in to see me in an extremely anxious state because he had just lost his job. A doctor had given him a tranquilizing drug, but I told him to stop taking it because I wanted to see clearly the kind of anxiety he was suffering.

"Since I've lost my job," he told me, "I've been so anxious and nervous I can't even sleep at night."

"Did they fire you?" I asked.

"No. I had a heart attack, and they retired me on a good disability pension. I'm living all right, nothing to worry about financially, but I can't stand sitting at home. I break out in cold sweats and start shaking. My wife says I should just enjoy myself, but I can't."

As we discussed his background, I learned he had lived all over the world and enjoyed a privileged status as an American employee in foreign countries.

"I just don't understand it," he said,

shaking his head. "I should be very comfortable now, but I'm not."

"No, you shouldn't be comfortable, given your background and personality," I said. "You're reacting very appropriately. You can't take this drug for the rest of your life — you'll die young if you do. Tell me, did you ever think of regarding that anxiety you're experiencing as a signal from God? He may be trying to tell you something here. He may be letting you know you're not doing what you should be doing."

"What do you mean?" he asked.

"You've been very active in the past, and now you're passive. Maybe you're too young to stop work. Are you ready to do nothing for the rest of your life?"

He shook his head. "I feel as though I'm in a wastepaper basket, as though I'm worthless."

"What did you want to do before you went into government service?"

He grinned. "I always wanted to go to law school, but I gave up that idea after I got my bachelor's degree."

"Does that still appeal to you?"

He looked at me in a funny way. "Strange you should say that, because I've been wishing lately that I had a law degree so I could set up a practice. I knew a lot of lawyers in government service who did just that after they left the government."

"Then why don't you go to law school now?" I asked. "Your government contacts and knowledge of the bureaucracy and its procedures would be invaluable."

That was one of my easiest cases. Ray applied to law school, got in, earned his law degree, and now has a thriving practice. He'll be a productive, vital person for years because he responded appropriately to his realistic feelings of anxiety, rather than trying to smother them with tranquilizers. The best antidote for this kind of anxiety is *constructive action*. You should help your spouse or friend pinpoint the source of his worry, and then encourage him to move forward and trust that God will guide him. As the Psalmist said, "Commit your fate to Yahweh, trust in him and he will act." (Psalm 37:5).

A priest I know from the Midwest,

Father Jerry, also experienced an attack of realistic anxiety because he allowed his ambition to achieve and move up in the Roman Catholic hierarchy to take precedence over his commitment to Christ. His main problem, he told me, was a fear that he was going to die soon, and I thought that was a strange thing for a priest to be worrying about.

"I'm on tranquilizers because I get so worried about death," he said. "It's ridiculous — I think I've had more cancer tests than anyone else in the world."

"And you're probably disappointed you didn't have cancer, right?" I said.

"Well, if I did have cancer, I suppose at least I'd know my worries were justified."

"Perhaps they *are* justified," I replied, "but not for the reasons you suspect."

As he began to open up to me about his life as a church leader, the story that unfolded was of a young seminarian who had felt a strong call to serve God but had gradually become enamored of the good life with friendly bishops and business executives. Highly intelligent and personable, Father Jerry was a prime candidate for higher church office. He liked to eat and drink well, and soon found himself entertaining an ambition to become a bishop, even a cardinal, and maybe even . . . who knows?

"Everything is going so well for me," he concluded. "I just can't understand why I should be so afraid about my health and about dying."

"There's a good reason why you should be afraid," I said. I then reminded him of the rich man Jesus described in Luke 12:16 - 21. This wealthy landowner made a financial killing on an abundant harvest, and the first thing he thought of was to build new barns so that he could store all his grain and worldly goods and live happily and worry-free for years. The problem was that he failed to consider God and the welfare of his own soul. He said to himself, " 'My soul, you have plenty of good things laid by for many years to come; take things easy, eat, drink, have a good time.' "

But God interrupted his grandiose, self-centered plans by declaring, " 'Fool! This very night the demand will be made for your soul; and this hoard of yours, whose will it be then?' "

Jesus concluded, " 'So it is when a man stores up treasure for himself in place of making himself rich in the sight of God.' "

After recounting this story, I related it to the priest's own situation: "The difference between you and this rich man is that he felt no anxiety about the fact that death might cut short all his worldly plans and ambitions. But God is tipping you off ahead of time with these feelings of anxiety. You've become devoted to the good life, and you sense there's a difference between what you are and what you should be. You've been spending most of your time with these big shots in the hierarchy and in the business community, but how much time have you been spending with the ordinary parishioners who are under the your care?"

"Not much," he admitted quietly.

"How many souls have you brought to the Lord in the past year?"

He shook his head. "None."

"You may become Pope, but you won't be happy," I said. "You're too concerned about moving up, succeeding in terms that have nothing to do with Christian values. Your priorities are messed up. Something inside you — the Spirit of God, I think — is telling you things are not the way they should be.''

''I think you're probably right,'' he said.

''So perhaps your anxiety is a healthy thing,'' I said. ''Perhaps God is using these agitated, frustrated feelings inside you to let you know that your values have shifted, that you're headed in the wrong direction since you felt that initial call from Him. You're more interested in the golf course or the upcoming trip to Bermuda than in the number of people you'll reach on Sunday morning with your homily. You're caught up in the achievement bag, and maybe God is trying to signal you that it's time to change course.''

''Maybe that's why I'm afraid of death,'' he observed.

''Exactly. It's more than death — it's the judgment of God that will follow death. If you know you're following God's will for your life, there's nothing to be afraid of, right?''

Father Jerry is well on his way toward *not* becoming a bishop now. He's in evangelical work, and he says he might even turn down the office of bishop if it's offered him. If he did take it, he'd be the kind of leader who would say, "Christ is running my diocese.'' I'm inclined to think he just might move up in the hierarchy, but with a transformed, Christ-like attitude toward his responsibilities. He's one of the best examples I know of a person who has found the profound truth of Jesus's saying, "For anyone who wants to save his life [or in Father Jerry's case, his career ambitions] will lose it; but anyone who loses his life for my sake will find it.'' (Matthew 16:25).

If a person is willing to take appropriate action, feelings of realistic anxiety can often be completely eliminated. But overcoming chronic or "free-floating'' anxiety can be a more complex matter. If a Christian is emotionally healthy, his trust in the power and comfort of God's Spirit can do much to eliminate worry.

Sometimes, though, a person's ego doesn't develop properly because of a failure of the parents to convey to a child the sense that he's worthwhile. The child gradually begins to feel hostility toward the parents because they don't seem to love him. Afraid that he won't be able to control the intense anger he feels, he bottles these feelings inside himself, consciously and unconsciously, and free-floating anxiety is the result.

Helen, a young registered nurse who was not a Christian, came to me with a mind full of anxieties. She lived in torture almost every day. If she opened a newspaper and read that a woman had been killed, she feard she also would be murdered. She was always afraid she'd lose her job, even though there was a great demand for nurses where she lived. Although she was an attractive single woman in her late twenties, boy friends didn't interest her because worry was a full-time job.

I could tell at the outset she was suffering from a classic case of free-floating anxiety, so I immediately turned the discussion toward her early experiences with her parents. Her father had been an alcoholic, and her mother was high-strung and very anxious. The mother spent most of her time fighting with the father or complaining about the way he abused her, and devoted little time to Helen.

"I really felt like I wasn't a very nice person," Helen told me. "I never seemed to be able to do anything right. Mostly, Mother just ignored me and Dad was usually too drunk to be aware that I was even around."

In the way they failed to relate to Helen, her parents communicated a lack of acceptance to her. As a result, she emerged from childhood with a weak ego, a sense that nothing she did or achieved would ever be quite up to par or acceptable to any authority figure. She also remembered feeling very angry toward her parents at different times because they wouldn't pay attention to her in the way other parents attended to their children. But her parents were too powerful, too God-like for her rage to have any effect if she vented it, so she learned to turn her anger back inside herself.

"Have you ever gotten serious about a young man?" I asked.

"Not really," she said. "Oh, I've had a couple of experiences. I went out with a few guys, had sex, but nothing came of it. They weren't getting very much."

"What do you mean?"

"I mean me. They didn't get much by having sex with me. What do I have to offer them?"

"Did you find anxiety increased after these affairs?" I asked. "Think about the last one. Do you remember worrying a lot after that about different things?"

She pondered for a moment and then said, "Yes, as a matter of fact, I did. I remember getting really panicky when I was reading the paper. I saw a story about a suicide, and I began to worry that I was going to kill myself. And then I read about someone killed in a car crash, and I started wondering whether I might die that way."

"What you were really doing," I explained, "was thinking anxious thoughts that would distract you from the anger and hostility you felt toward this guy who abused you and then dropped you. You thought you might kill yourself, but your subconscious was actually saying, 'I might kill this guy.' The fear of violent death in a car accident was also related to your anger toward your boy friend. And all this hostility has it roots in the anger you never were able to express toward your parents. The reason you can't allow yourself to think about this anger and express it is that you're afraid you won't be able to control it. You have what we call a weak or damaged ego, a sense you're not a good person and not strong enough to manage these violent feelings that well up inside you. All this anxiety that's making your life miserable stems from your basic notion, which developed in childhood, that you're not as good as other people."

"I'm not so sure it's wrong for me to feel that way," she said sadly. "I'm not so sure I *am* a worthwhile person."

"But that's where you're dead wrong!" I replied enthusiastically. "I'm an objective person, and I can see a lot of good — no, *superior* things about you. You're a very competent person, and you're able to exercise much more control over your environment than you think you can. When you learn how to take charge of your life a little better, your ego will get stronger and you'll lose a lot of these anxieties."

At this point, I moved from my role of attentive listener to become the comforting, supportive mother that Helen never had. I also began to joke with her about her symptoms — "Did you find something good in the paper to worry about today? I'll tell you, I got up early this morning and marked a few good stories for you to check out if you overlooked them. . . . " She gradually projected onto me many of the feelings she had developed toward her own parents and tested me to determine whether or not I really liked and accepted her.

I canceled an appointment with her one day because I had to be out of town, and when we met two weeks after, she accused me of not wanting to see her. "I'll bet you weren't out of town at all," she sulked.

"I'll bet you were with another patient you liked better."

I could see she was trying to fit into the role of the little child, waiting for her parents to come in drunk at night. But I wouldn't allow that: "You're giving me a hard time, even though you know I'm not trying to avoid you," I said gently. "Believe me, if I didn't want to see you again, I'd tell you not to come around any more. I have too many other patients waiting to get into this office to play games like that. But I *am* seeing you today, and I'll see you again next week, so quit getting so upset about nothing!"

As I continued to be supportive, she improved and her ego underwent a re-education, but I always had to be on my guard because she had an arsenal of subtle weapons to test me.

"What if I went beserk and tore your diplomas down and ripped this office apart?" she asked one day.

"You don't have to be frightened about that because I assure you I'm not going to sit by and let you do that," I said firmly. "You might end up with a broken arm if you try anthing."

That gave her a great deal of security because she knew I was strong enough to exercise control over her. Her parents had never given her any control, and she wanted to make sure I was different. She had been one of those children who had experienced a great deal of absolute freedom because her parents hadn't cared what happened to her. At a young age she could stay out until extremely late hours. Other kids envied her, but she felt nobody really cared. To overcome her feelings that her parents were indifferent, she made up a story that she had an extremely strict mother and father who would punish her severely if she didn't get in early in the evening. It was all fiction, but at least it made her feel better.

In the turbulence of our relationship, Helen finally came to believe that I accepted her and saw something good in her, though she couldn't understand exactly what. But her unconscious attempts to force me into the destructive, abusive role of her parents continued. One day she came in for her session in a low-cut blouse and seductive, form-fitting skirt. She was an attractive young woman, and the import of the message she was trying to convey wasn't lost on me.

In case I had missed the point, however, she came right out with it after we had talked for a couple of minutes. "I don't feel like sitting in this stuffy room for a whole hour," she said in a sultry tone. "Why don't we go out and talk over a drink? As a matter of fact, I know a nice bar up the road . . . it's part of a motel, and after the drinks, who knows. . . ."

She was looking me straight in the eye. Despite all her negative feelings about herself, she was obviously aware that her sexual attractiveness gave her a certain power over men. Some psychoanalysts have fallen into the trap of convincing themselves that having sex with a patient will enhance the cure. In fact, all considerations of Christian morality aside, sexual involvement always *destroys* any progress the therapist may have made. I've run into cases where suicide attempts have resulted when psychotherapists have used sex as a pretense for treatment.

Helen obviously was inviting me to violate the trust relationship we had built up. She knew where I stood on adultery, and if I had gotten involved with her, I would have been betraying my own values as well as our relationship. She had precipitated a major crisis, and I had to show her I could control my own feelings with a strong ego.

"You're an attractive woman, Helen, but I can't go out with you because I love you."

Puzzled, she asked, "What do you mean?"

"My relationship with God helps me overcome my natural feelings as a healthy male in a situation like this," I continued. "If I got involved with you outside this office, that would hurt you, and it wouldn't be showing love. When two people have sex, it should be the beginning, not the end."

After this conversation, she realized it was possible to have a relationship with someone and not be abused. I behaved differently from her parents and selfish boy friends, who had convinced her she was a worthless person, suitable only for exploitation. Helen's improvement, which was rooted in the re-education of her ego, was possible only because we had a warm and loving relationship. The fact that I accepted her and showed my concern for her was the biggest factor in undercutting the deep feelings of hostility and anxiety that wracked her personality. When I establish a relationship like this, I can't help loving the person. One of the hardest things for me is "graduation day" — the day when discussions and therapy end, and the person leaves me to try an independent life.

I welcomed Helen's last shot at me as her substitute parent because I knew that ultimately her ability to master worry and anxiety would depend on spiritual, rather than emotional development. When I first mentioned I was a Christian, she tried to taunt me sometimes by yelling, "Christ!" because she knew that would provoke me.

Finally, I decided that enough was enough and that she was actually expecting me to exercise some form of parental control. "Helen," I said sternly. "I'm going to forbid you to use the name of

Christ like that in my presence. That's a name I use only in prayer and reverence, and out of respect for my feelings and for Christ Himself, I'm going to forbid you to talk like that.''

''Oh yeah?'' she retorted defiantly. ''And what will you do if I *do* talk like that? Throw me out?''

''That's something I'll have to consider, yes.''

I knew that our relationship was solid by this time and that she'd be pleading to come back if I told her I wouldn't see her any more. I had become a parent who cared by saying, ''I have values and I'm not going to put up with this any longer.'' She began to refer jokingly to my office as ''Salvation Army headquarters,'' and said she felt like she should put a nickel on my drum every time she came in. I always laughed, and sometimes said, ''Amen to that, sister.''

A couple of weeks after this confrontation over her blasphemous language, she walked in and cried, ''Hey, have you gone completely crazy?''

''What are you talking about? I asked.

"Why have you started putting Bibles in the waiting room all of a sudden? Is this turning into some kind of a church?"

I smiled and said, "They've been in there for the past year."

"Come on! Why didn't I notice them before?"

"Because your ego has almost healed, your anxiety has dissipated, and you're more interested in examining things outside yourself. You'll probably find, if you haven't already, that you need to look for some meaning in life outside yourself. One reason that you noticed the Bibles may be that they represent the possibility of that kind of meaning."

"You mean God?" she asked.

"Yes, God."

"I don't think God can love me."

"Yes He can. He *does* love you. He loves you this much," I said, and held my arms out wide, in the form of a cross. At that, Helen broke down and cried. I patted her on the back, and she put her head on my shoulder. When she moved away, my shirt was wet with her tears. She's been moving slowly and cautiously toward Christ, but only she and God know where she'll finally find a spiritual resting place. The satisfaction that I have is to know that the main block to her spirituality — the horrendous, free-floating anxiety that had almost destroyed her naturally beautiful personality — has been removed.

Anxiety, depression, and boredom are the Terrible Triumvirate of emotional ills that beset all of us to some degree at one time or another. We'll be referring back to each of these disturbances because they frequently pop up as the unpleasant companions of other personality problems. Now let's turn to one of the most important and sensationalized of those other problems — sex.

Chapter Eight

Toward a Healthy Sexuality

When I ask my patients, "How's your sex life?" here are some of the answers I get:

"Sex is something a woman has to put up with."

"Sexual pleasure is the most important thing in a marriage."

"All men are animals in bed."

"My wife is always too tired."

"We got divorced because our sex drives weren't compatible."

"Sex is the source of all sin."

"It's such a, well, a *dirty* thing, don't you think?"

Our preoccupation with sex has caused a natural, beautiful function to degenerate into the source of many of our psychological ills. We are taught that if we cannot experience this pleasure to the fullest, our lives will be incomplete, so we become eager to master every possible sexual variation, inside and outside marriage. Our eagerness is so overwhelming that it's transformed into anxiety, which in turn may prevent us from enjoying even the simplest sexual pleasures.

Christians who escape these self-destructive sexual obsessions of our culture confront another roadblock to a healthy sexuality. Roman Catholicism has been infected by the heresy, Jansenism, which taught an un-Christian dualistic message — that spiritual or nonmaterial things are good, and physical, bodily, and sexual things are bad. Protestants have had the same problem with the Victorian distortions of Puritanism. With these deep-rooted misconceptions, it's a wonder that any contemporary Christian has developed a normal, pleasurable, yet well-controlled sex life.

What is the proper approach for the Christian to take to sexual relationships? The Scriptures and centuries of church tradition stand unequivocally for the idea that sex should take place inside the marriage relationship. Adultery, fornication, and homosexuality are inconsistent with the natural order of creation that God has established. (See Romans 1:18 - 27; Matthew 16:19; Leviticus 20:13.)

But just because God has provided a definite framework for expressing sexuality, that doesn't mean Christians are prohibited from enjoying themselves within the proper bounds. On the contrary, the Bible says that God acknowledged that everything He created was good, and this divine stamp of approval must include human sex drives. (Genesis 1:31; I Timothy 4:4). The Apostle Paul said that ". . . if they cannot control the sexual urges, they should get married, since it is better to be married than to be tortured." (1 Corinthians 7:9). Although Paul said he preferred to remain single, he certainly didn't fall into the dualistic trap of regarding the body, including the sexual functions, as bad.

I conclude from these teachings that sex is a good thing and should be enjoyed creatively within the bounds of marriage. But just how creative should a Christian get? A woman asked a priest I know, "What is and what is not permitted in sex relations in marriage?"

He replied, "If you pay for the main event, you're entitled to the preliminaries."

Sexual intercourse and sexual foreplay between a husband and wife are basically good and can help build a strong love relationship. The only limits I would set are that the couple should avoid those acts which might hurt or repulse one or the other partner. There has been a great deal written and said recently in Christian circles about how wives can titillate their husbands with sexy costumes and various other techniques. I think eroticism can be healthy and can enhance sexual pleasure. But in the last analysis it's not so much what you wear or how many mirrors you use, but the attitude you present. I had one woman tell me she sometimes wished her husband would not return home in the evening. Although he was loving and considerate toward her, she almost preferred that he'd end up in an accident and have to spend the night in the hospital, rather than come home and be interested in sexual intercourse. This woman suffered from a disturbed state of mind that no costume can cure.

Unhealthy attitudes toward sex may result in one of the two most common sexual ills that men and women face in our society — frigidity and impotence. Frigidity involves an inability on the part of the wife to relax and open herself, emotionally and physically, to sexual penetration by her husband. Frigidity has no influence on the ability to have children, but there is little or no enjoyment during intercourse and frigid women rarely, if ever, experience an orgasm. Impotence in men most frequently manifests itself in chronic inability to have or maintain an erection, or in premature ejaculation. To understand the causes of these problems and the ways Christian love can provide solutions, let's take a look at some concrete illustrations.

1. *Frigidity*. Frigidity in a woman is not necessarily the same thing as failure to

have on orgasm. The current sex gurus assume that the orgasm is the ultimate goal and that a lack of orgasms indicates an unhealthy sex life. My clinical experience has demonstrated to me that this assumption is untrue. One woman, whose attitude was typical of many women I know, came in with a marital problem, and at one point I asked her, "Do you enjoy sex?"

"Yes," she replied. "But I rarely have an orgasm."

"What do you enjoy about sex, then?" I said.

"The closeness to my husband, the warmth of having him near me. I love him, and it makes me feel good to give him pleasure."

When a woman like this straightens out her other problems, it's likely she will have an orgasm, but it's not essential to her sexual happiness. If you or someone you know is in this category, there's no need to create unnecessary dissatisfaction or unhappiness by overemphasizing orgasms. They will often begin to occur more frequently as both sexual partners mature, and get to know each other's needs and physical sensitivities.

Sometimes, though, everything about the sex act seems repulsive or unpleasant to a woman, and this problem calls for an intelligent application of Christian love. Margot, a middle-aged Christian housewife, made an appointment with me because of what she described as "a total state of alienation from my husband. We hardly talk to each other. He comes home from work, slams the door, doesn't even kiss me. He doesn't seem to be glad to see me at all. Just grunts a few words at dinner and then heads directly for the TV set with a couple of cans of beer. He ignores me all night."

"How about your sexual relationship?" I asked.

"He's not too interested. I'm worried he may be involved with another woman. I get so mad thinking about it that when he *does* want to have intercourse, I sometimes just turn him off. I'm not going to play second fiddle to some other woman!"

"Have you ever thought you might be

holding yourself off from him sexually and that's the main cause of your problem?" I asked.

"No way," she said. "I dish out what he needs, and he ought to be happy with what he gets. I can't take it more than twice a week — that's too much, as far as I'm concerned."

"Do you ever have the feeling you just want him to get it over with?"

"Sure — all the time. It's not really much fun for me."

"Do you think sex is dirty?"

"Not exactly. Just not much fun — part of God's curse on women after He threw them out of the Garden of Eden, I suppose. I can put up with it."

During the rest of our conversation that day, we discussed Margot's relationships with her parents because I suspected that her main problem stemmed from her early childhood. I learned she had a tremendous amount of hostility toward her mother, who was a very exploitative woman. The mother had been overt in her displays of affection and warmth, but had used this loving facade as a mask for her manipulations. She in effect demanded that Margot not grow up, that she remain a little girl with unquestioning loyalty to her parents. Her mother continued to exercise this controlling influence even after Margot got married. The older woman would often call her daughter at midnight for no particular reason, and when the phone rang at that time, there was a strong possibility that some sexual activity was underway. The mother, in other words, was actually trying to reach out and manage Margot's married sex life.

Margot transferred her feeling about her mother to her husband, Bob. She regarded Bob's occasional sexual demands as exploitative because exploitation was the main characteristic she had known in her own family. But while she had been unable to express hostility toward her mother, she tried to take out her anger on Bob by denying him sex.

I suspected part of the problem lay with Bob himself, so I asked him to come in for a visit and found he had serious emotional problems of his own. His mother had shown him little love, and he was grateful for even the slight affection he received from Margot. Together, they had re-created their own childhood patterns by transferring their feelings toward their mothers to each other. They had reached an interpersonal balance — or "homeostasis," as professional therapists call it — in which they were attempting unsuccessfully to re-enact their youthful traumas and heal their emotional wounds.

Because Margot's frigidity was deeply rooted in her relationship with her mother, I knew I had to become a substitute mother in order to begin the healing process. As I assumed this role, Margot immediately began to test me. She failed to pay her therapy fee for two straight weeks, and when I reminded her about it, she said, "Oh, I'll take care of it next time."

My secretary presented her with the bill for the three back sessions the next week, and she got angry at the relatively large amount. "You're just trying to use me, like everybody else!" she cried when she came into my office. "Look at this bill! Since when am I supposed to pay this much?"

"You haven't paid me for three sessions now," I replied.

"I just don't know what I'm going to do!" she continued without really hearing me. "I don't know where to turn any more!"

"Margot," I replied. "Don't you see what you're doing?"

"What do you mean?"

"You're transferring some of your feelings toward your mother to me, and that's fine — that's important for us to be able to cure your problem. But you also think I'm going to exploit you as your mother has done, and you're wrong about that. I'm not exploiting you. It's just that you've unconsciously allowed your bill to accumulate to a large sum so that you can convince yourself I'm abusing you."

She had no answer for my interpretation, so I knew she sensed some validity in it. "You're doing a similar thing with your husband," I continued. "You turn him down two or three times in bed, and he begins to burn with passion. Then when you finally have intercourse, he's so frustrated that he concentrates on satisfying his own needs and perhaps shows less compassion or gentleness than you'd like. You in effect force him to behave in a way that you can interpret as exploitative."

"That's a lie!" she exploded. She was furious at me and almost walked out of the office. But finally, after she had calmed down, she saw the truth in what I was saying. The hostility that she expressed toward me, her substitute mother, was the first step in the healing process. Soon, she was able to express the anger and hostility which resulted from her mother's interference in her life. After venting this anger, Margot learned to resolve it and her relationship with her mother improved and matured. If she had stayed angry at me or her mother, that would have been poor therapy and there would have been no possibility of healing. As it was, the resolution of her childhood problems helped her to come alive sexually with her husband. She actually began to look forward to bedtime — and her mother never called at midnight again.

Margot's progress in her sex life also produced positive results in her other relationships. Her children got the fringe benefits of having a more loving, outgoing mother. And her Christian faith, and her dealings with other Christians became a more joyous experience as well. Sex, she finally understood, was something created by God and was basically a *good* thing, when we learn to use it properly. Her internalized hostility toward her mother, and the resulting frigidity, had prevented her from understanding that the sex drive is a gift from God which should enhance marital relationships.

2. Impotence. I've mentioned that sexual impotence in a man can be manifested in a variety of ways, including an inability to get and hold an erection, an abnormal lack of sexual desire, or a tendency toward premature ejaculation. Some men, concerned about whether their sex drives are normal, have asked me, "How often should the normal married couple have intercourse?" I always reply that there is no set number of times per week that should be regarded as healthy or unhealthy. But if a husband and wife have sex only once every two weeks or once a month during their sexually active years, I would want to know why they don't get together more. Something unhealthy may be happening to their marriage. On the other hand, if someone says, "We missed last week, but then we had sex three times this week," I wouldn't regard that as something to get concerned about. Some "sexperts" cite averages — three times a week before you're thirty-five, twice a week in your forties, and so on — but I think this approach can create unnecessary anxieties if, in the course of the career rat race, the husband or wife is too tired to perform during a given week.

Some men, though, avoid intercourse for long periods of time and blame their wives without even being aware that their problem may be in themselves. Take the case of Mike, a Christian in his late thirties, who told me his marriage was in trouble.

"I want to talk to you about my wife," he began. "I haven't had intercourse with her for seven years, and I want to know what's wrong with her."

My jaw sagged slightly at this revelation,

but I quickly recovered and asked, "Do you have a girl friend?"

"No, I've never been unfaithful to my wife."

I sensed that he had at least as serious a problem as his wife because he was apparently suffering from a degree of impotency without knowing it. As we talked, Mike told me his wife's father was living with them and "he's like God to her." From his description, I could see that the wife was involved in an incestuous bind with her father and that the two of them were cutting Mike out. He had been too weak a person to cause a crisis and clear the air.

Mike's underlying problem, as it turned out, had been an overdemanding mother, and he had developed a great deal of hostility toward females. He had learned to fight against his mother by sulking and withholding love from her. Now his wife had taken his mother's place and he was withholding his sexuality. Mike's father, a prominent minister, had contributed to the problem by stressing to his son that human sexuality was a bad and dangerous thing. The guilt feelings that consequently surrounded Mike's attitudes toward sex made intercourse the easiest thing for him to deny his wife.

In the unhealthy situation that had developed in his home, his wife's father had taken the place of his own authoritarian father and his wife had become, in Mike's eyes, his dominating mother. For all practical purposes, he was still living with his own mother and father, and his spiritual and emotional growth had been stunted.

"You're going to have to rock the boat at home," I told him.

"What do you mean?" Mike asked nervously.

"I mean, you're going to have to create a crisis and get some of your feelings of hostility out into the open. You're withholding sex from your wife because she's taken the place of your mother, and you've helped drive her back to this unhealthy, close relationship with her father. Your marriage doesn't have a chance if you don't assert yourself."

He finally decided to confront his wife

with the issue. When she lashed out at him one day for no apparent reason, he retorted, "What's wrong with you! Why are you always ranking me out? Things are going to have to change in this house!"

His wife was, for once, speechless, and her father, who had been sitting off to one side, stepped into the fray: "What are you saying to my daughter?" he shouted. "She's a good girl."

"She's not such a good girl, and you keep out of this!" Mike said.

After the argument ended, with the father turning his back and the wife running to the bedroom in tears, Mike felt less sure of himself. He was tempted to back down and revert to his old, passive self, but he held his ground until he could see me again.

"This is very upsetting," he said. "I don't know if I can go through with it."

"Of course it's upsetting!" I replied. "Your wife and father-in-law are comfortable with their situation, even if it's destroying your marriage. They really don't realize what's happening. But you do, and you have a responsibility to take

235

the lead in straightening things out. You're going to have to become the strong person in the family. You have what it takes. Now stick to it!"

By building up his ego, I provided him with a source of strength to break through the neurotic atmosphere in his household. The therapy, which had led to turmoil, finally resulted in healing. Mike's guilt feelings about sex gradually left him, and the Spirit of God was given a less cluttered emotional framework in which to operate. He found that he could relate to women much better than ever before. And because I had stressed a Christian sense of responsibility in his dealings with his relatives, he retained a value system which prevented him from becoming sexually involved with another woman. His wife gradually adjusted to his more independent, self-assured personality, and their belated sex life began to blossom.

If your husband or friend has a problem with impotence, the chances are it's not as serious as Mike's seven-year period of abstinence. But regardless of how mild the malady is, you will need to show as much understanding and love as I did to Mike because impotence is especially difficult for a man to discuss and frustrating to try to cure. A man's self-image is often tied closely to his sexual performance, and sexual inadequacy can result in distortions of other personality characteristics. It's especially hard for a wife to help a husband cure his impotency without outside help because she, like Mike's wife, may be contributing unconsciously to the problem. My advice to wives would be to search your own personality for quirks that may be threatening your husband's masculinity and sense of authority. Then eliminate these deficiencies before you try to help him. If his impotence fails to improve despite such love and ego support, seek help from a third party, a professional counselor.

3. *Masturbation and the lustful imagination.* Masturbation is an issue that arises during adolescence, and if parents don't take a healthy approach to it, both in boys and girls, the future sex life of the young person can be damaged. My own

advice is to approach the problem with general, but not too specific moral guidance. *And the parent of the opposite sex should stay out of any discussion on masturbation.* I've treated young boys whose mothers examined their sheets every night to see if they had stained the bed during a "wet dream," or in involuntary emission while the boy is asleep. Technically, these nocturnal emissions aren't masturbations at all, but some mothers attack any display of sexuality and create unnecessary anxiety in their sons. It's unfair for any parent to blame a son for wet dreams over which he has no control. If the issue of masturbation comes up, the father should discuss the matter with the son, and the mother with the daughter. Otherwise, there is a danger of creating sexual feelings in the child toward the parent of the opposite sex. I talked to one boy who didn't know what masturbation was until his mother accused him of doing it. She in effect instructed him in auto-stimulation, and he began to masturbate regularly, with his mother as his fantasized sexual object.

Masturbation and wet dreams are inevitable in all normal young people, Christians as well as non-Christians. The most serious problem with masturbation for a single person, is to masturbate excessively, say five or six or more times a day, and to make the sex organ the primary focus of life. Uncontrolled masturbation may also plague a married person and hinder his sex life with his spouse. If a married man masturbates once or twice a day, it's likely that his testicles will be empty and his sexual desire low when he climbs into bed with his wife at night. This situation may put their sexual relationship in jeopardy. Such masturbation may indicate an infantile approach to life, an inability to form a mature relationship.

One of the saddest examples I've encountered of this obsession with masturbation involved the husband of a beautiful young woman who came to me for advice. She had been married for six months and had a warm and inviting personality, but her husband had been unable to have intercourse with her because he was an obsessive masturbator. When he climbed into bed, he reverted to a little boy and acted childishly, even to the point of using baby talk. In the middle of the night, he'd say, "Give me a drink of wawa — I thirsty."

On their first night of marriage, she waited and waited in bed while her husband was in the bathroom. She learned later that he was masturbating in there. Unable to fulfill the role of man, he remained unemployed, and she finally had the marriage annulled on the ground that the relationship had never been consummated.

One activity that is often associated with masturbation is sexual fantasies. Such flights of the imagination are sometimes condemned because of Jesus' teaching in the Sermon on the Mount: "You have learnt how it was said: *You must not commit adultery*. But I say this to you: if a man looks at a woman lustfully, he has already committed adultery with her in his heart." (Matthew 5:27 - 28). I don't believe that Jesus had in mind the situation where a man walks down the street, spots

240

a beautiful woman and thinks, "Hmm, she's really good-looking." Instead, He seemed to be referring to the detailed mental image that turns into an internal X-rated movie and threatens to preoccupy your mind with sexual thoughts, or perhaps encourages you to consider taking steps to get the woman into bed.

Sometimes an undisciplined fantasy life can hinder a good sex relationship in marriage. If you imagine, on a regular basis, that you're having intercourse with someone else's husband when it's your own husband in your arms, you can assume that something is wrong with your attitude. An occasional fantasy of this type is not serious, but if it becomes a constant part of your sex life, it may be a signal that you're very angry with your husband (or wife). Your subconscious mind is saying that, for some reason, your husband or wife doesn't turn you on, and this is an indication that you should take a hard look at your marriage, find the problem and correct it.

I'm reminded of a story one of my patients told me about a dream he had.

He had been having unsatisfactory sex with his wife, and other women had been tempting him. He dreamed that he walked in on his wife and found her in the act of intercourse with another man.

"What was your feeling in the dream?" I asked.

"I went over to the guy, tapped him on the shoulder and said, 'Hey, listen, I *gotta* do it. What's your excuse?' "

This dream may seem funny at first, but it indicates that the man didn't love his wife. He had a serious problem which related back to his lack of love for his mother in childhood. We had to explore this parental relationship before he could understand why he felt as he did and begin to repair his marriage.

Excessive fantasies and masturbation can often be cured by asking God to give you, your spouse, or your friend the *will power* to overcome these bad habits and temptations. Psychotherapists sometimes forget that parental and environmental influences may only be a small part of a personality problem. Just saying, "No, I won't do it," and sticking by that decision may be a better answer than hour after hour of introspection and therapy.

For example, if a businessman is on a trip away from home, he may check into a hotel and see copies of sex magazines at the hotel newsstand. If he buys a copy of one of these pornographic publications, his fantasies will begin to roam freely and perhaps even dominate his mind; and he'll be easier prey for the inevitable prostitutes in the neighborhood. He can say no at any stage of this movement from fantasy to infidelity, but it's easier to cut off temptation at the outset by just turning away from the newsstand.

Paul's words to the Christians at Ephesus seem appropriate here: "Among you there must be not even a mention of fornication or impurity in any of its forms, or promiscuity: this would hardly become the saints! There must be no coarseness, or salacious talk and jokes — all this is wrong for you; raise your voices in thanksgiving instead. For you can be quite certain that nobody who actually indulges in fornication or impurity or promiscuity . . . can inherit anything of the kingdom of God. . . . [Have] nothing to do with the futile works of darkness but [expose] them by contrast. The things which are done in secret are things that people are ashamed even to speak of"; (Ephesians 5:3 - , 11 - 12). The apostle suggests that many salacious activities are under our control. We should exercise our wills in pushing away immorality, and trust God to sustain us in our resolve.

If you feel led by God to point out to a friend that his sexual activities are contrary to traditional Christian morality, be sure you have your biblical and theological agruments straight. And above all, avoid a pharisaical, judgmental approach. Your focus should be on healing the emotional problem and its outward manifestations, not on assuming God's role as the ultimate arbiter of right and wrong. If a person knows you're a Christian, he'll expect you to be moralistic, rather than compassionate and understanding. Unless you can prove to him that you care before you start tossing Bible verses around, you won't be able to help. A prostitute came to see me, and the first thing she said was,

"I know you're going to preach to me."

"I have no reason to preach," I replied. "I'm concerned about your self-destruction. I see a beautiful person who is going to waste. You must feel that way too, or you wouldn't have come to see me."

When she saw I was interested in relating to her as an individual, rather than merely as a potential convert, a trust was established and therapy could begin in earnest. I'm not saying you should soft-pedal those things which are clearly right and wrong, especially if such an approach seems important to the healing process. Just be careful about assuming condescending, self-righteous attitudes, which will prevent you from demonstrating true Christian love.

4. Steer clear of the sex therapists. As you try to resolve your own sexual problems and those of your loved ones, let me give one word of warning: beware of popular sex therapy. These "sexperts," or self-styled experts in the mechanical techniques of sex stress the use of oils, vibrators, and a variety of coital positions as the answer to most sex problems. They often ignore the basic cause of the difficulty, which more often than not is an inability or unwillingness on the part of one or both spouses to show or accept love. If a husband is moving too quickly during the sex act, the sexperts might tell him to caress her, rub in a certain spot for a certain number of minutes. But I would tell him he had a basic problem in relating to his wife. If the husband's approach is boom! and it's all over, he may be feeling hostility toward his wife or toward women in general. Foreplay is important, but warm, effective stimulation techniques will follow naturally after underlying hostilities are removed.

Most of the sex manuals that come out these days have the same problem — too much method and not enough genuine love. A husband whom I know said, "I use this book on sexology, but we still don't have good sex relations."

I asked, "When you make love, in what hand do you hold the book?"

He laughed, but the point sank in. He

was focusing on the technique and not on the relationship.

If you counsel someone other than your spouse about sex problems, it's also extremely important to be aware of the dangers of getting sexually involved yourself. That has been one of the biggest mistakes that many secular psychotherapists have made: The supposed experts let their own sexual problems get wrapped up in their therapy, and an ordinary, garden-variety affair is the result. These therapists convince themselves that they can effect a cure by hopping onto the analytic couch with their client. But the mechanistic philosophy which underlies popular sex therapy ignores the fact that man has a spirit, and not just five physical senses.

The professional or lay therapist who gets involved in sex with the person he's counseling is either rationalizing or being deceitful. I had one Christian woman who came to me in a panic. She had seen a psychiatrist who told her that she had a number of sexual hang-ups and that the first step in correcting them was to take off her clothes. She undressed for him, and he said, "Now I'm going to teach you how to masturbate." She was so frightened she almost ran out of his office without her clothes.

Exploitation, selfishness, and incompetence are the only appropriate descriptions for would-be counselors who engage in such practices. The danger for you as a potential counselor, is that you can inadvertently fall into this same trap if you're not aware of the pitfalls in dealing with a person of the opposite sex. As you get to know the individual, he'll become more and more attractive. Every part of you, including your sex drive, will begin to respond. To control these impulses and keep the relationship at a healthy sexual distance, it's important to be careful of the way you schedule your meetings. Don't arrange to meet him late at night, or in a secluded spot where your desires can overcome your better judgment.

I've known clergymen who, without even being conscious of what they were doing, would give their last appointment to the most appealing female. Ministers are sitting ducks for this kind of mistake because they have their minds on many things other than pastoral counseling. They get tired at the end of the day and need pleasant companionship. If a parishioner in need of counseling can supply this need, the clergyman may subconsciously move toward that person at the most attractive time and place.

One very pretty ex-nun was frightened out of her wits by an unwise pastor at a church she started attending. She let him know she was having some problems with her faith, and he arranged to see her at 10 P.M. at her home. When he didn't show up by eleven, she assumed he had forgotten and got ready for bed. But then the doorbell rang. She ran to answer it in her negligee and bathrobe, and there stood the minister. She was very uncomfortable during the interview, and the longer he stayed, the more scared she became. Finally, at nearly 1:00 A.M., he left. She called me the next day and cried, "Doctor, what's wrong with me? I'm trying to understand what God wants of me, but then I get into a situation like this!"

"There's nothing wrong with you," I replied. "The problem is with that minister. I know him, so I'll give him a call and see what he had in mind."

The pastor claimed he didn't realize how late it was until he looked at his watch on the way out. But I knew he was having some difficulty in his own married life and was allowing himself, perhaps subconsciously, to cast about for sympathy and love outside his home. In psychoanalytic terms, the minister was getting enmeshed in "countertransference" with the person he was counseling. In other words, instead of just playing the role of the Good Parent with the young woman, he began to use her to resolve some of his own personal problems.

No counselor — psychoanalyst, clergyman, or Christian lay person — should assume he's above this countertransference trap. Sex counseling sometimes involves tremendous temptations, and situations that aggravate this temptation should be avoided at all costs. The best rule of thumb I know for helping a person with sexual problems was stated by the Apostle Paul in his letter to the Romans: "Do not let your love be a pretence, but sincerely prefer good to evil. Love each other as much as brothers should, and have a profound respect for each other." (Romans 12:9 - 10). If more therapists followed these guidelines, sex might cease to provoke so many emotional upsets in our society and might become what God always meant it to be — an enjoyable manifestation of marital love.

One topic which I've avoided in this chapter is homosexuality because I believe it deserves special treatment. With the rise of the outspoken Gay Liberation movement and agitation by civil rights activists for laws to eliminate discrimination against homosexuals, church leaders and professional psychotherapists are feeling considerable pressure to accept homosexuality as a moral and psychologically normal state of existence. This attitude has thrown many homosexuals who want to become heterosexuals into a quandary. Should they attempt to alter their sexual preferences into a socially more normal pattern, or should they try to be satisfied with liaisons involving their own sex? This question is the crux of the gay dilemma.

Chapter Nine

The Gay Dilemma

Homosexuals in our society are sinking into a quagmire of moral and emotional confusion. Militant gay leaders tell them they should come out of their closets and declare their sexual preferences publicly. Some church leaders argue that traditional Judaeo-Christian taboos against homosexuality are no longer applicable. The American Psychiatric Association has even removed homosexuality from its former designation as a mental disorder. To my mind, that would be like the American Cancer Society saying that cancer is no longer a disease.

Most of the homosexuals I've dealt with can't bring themselves to accept their condition as normal. Try as they may, they can't find happiness with a lover of the same sex. Something that transcends contemporary cultural and popular theological arguments seems wrong. I've had too much success in treating homosexuals to believe they should abandon the hope of becoming heterosexuals. Those who want to change, can change. And those who choose to remain homosexuals face the constant danger of falling into transient, primarily physical relationships.

As Christians, we can't accept the sexual outlets that the gay community has chosen. The Old Testament seers, the Apostle Paul, and all the subsequent molders of church tradition have been too explicit in stating that God's program for proper human relationships prohibits this practice. (See Leviticus 18:22; 20:13; Romans 1:26 - 27.) Pure and simple, it's sin, or transgression of God's moral law. But even if we can't condone what they're doing, we can still have a ministry to homosexuals. We should establish a friendship, show love and allow the Spirit of God to help them through us, just as,

254

we would deal with any other emotionally disturbed acquaintance.

The homosexual who wants to be helped will usually express some dissatisfaction with his way of life, and you should take that as a signal to help. Malcolm, a teacher at a Christian college, arranged to see me after a series of violent incidents made him fearful for his job and even for his life. He had developed an enviable reputation as a young professor, and had chosen to keep his homosexuality secret because he knew that, with the Christian orientation of his school, he would lose his job if the college administration found out about him.

"I'm not really so worried about my homosexuality," he began in an off-hand way. "I'm just worried about what's going on inside my head, making me destroy myself. I went out the other night, cruised around, picked up a kid — big, good-looking fellow about nineteen or twenty, I guess. We had something to drink and drove off to park for a while in a cemetery. But then the lights went out. I don't remember anything else until I woke up on the ground several hours later with a big gash in my head. Apparently, the kid hit me over the head with a bottle when I wasn't looking, and he took all my money. Now that shook me up."

"I can imagine," I murmured.

"Another time, I was sitting in my office in the college, and the police came in and asked if I had a certain color car with such and such a license plate. I said, 'Sure, that's my car. What's happened?' The cop just looked at me in a funny way and said, 'Nothing, we're just interested if that's your car,' and then they walked out. Now wasn't that weird?"

"Apparently, they were putting you on notice that they knew about you," I observed.

"I thought of that," Malcolm said. "Maybe they saw me pick up one of those kids on the main street next to the college. And you know, that panicked me. My whole career is in jeopardy. I can't figure out why everything seems to be working against me."

"The way you're putting yourself in these compromising positions, it seems inevitable to me you'll eventually be found out."

"Oh, oh, here it comes," he said sarcastically. "I didn't know what I was getting into when I saw that sign on your front door, CHRISTIAN INSTITUTE FOR PSYCHOTHERAPEUTIC STUDIES, but it's getting clearer now. I suppose the next thing is for you tell me I'm a sinner and I've got to stop being a homosexual."

"I'm not primarily concerned with your homosexuality, which is only a symptom of a much more serious problem," I said. "You've acquired a tremendous education at a great sacrifice, and now you're about to throw it all away. I'd like to know what's causing this self-destructive tendency inside you. At the rate you're going, you'll either be killed or arrested. Your whole reputation is at stake."

"As far as I'm concerned, the underlying problem is the way society treats homosexuals," he retorted.

"It's not that," I said. "If you really wanted to practice homosexuality, you'd get a mature partner and do it in some way that's not obvious. But here you are, cruising around your college, picking up tough kids you don't even know in locations where you're sure to be seen."

As we delved into his background, I learned that his father had died when he was quite young. He had started sleeping with his mother after his father's death, and continued to sleep with her until he was fifteen years old. There was no sex play between them; but, inevitably, Malcolm was stimulated. You can imagine the conflict this situation created in him. His personality development stopped for all practical purposes while he was in puberty.

Malcolm broke down and cried as he told me of his adolescence and how he denied and suppressed the sexual feelings he felt towards his mother. He couldn't refuse to sleep with her at that age because she had rendered him emotionally helpless. She imposed her own strong ego on his so that she could control and manipulate him.

When he finally tried dating some girls in high school, he found he wasn't attracted to them. His subconscious was saying, *I'm not interested in women because my mother is a woman and I'm not interested in my mother*. The only remaining outlet for his sexual urges was other men, and his homosexual experience began at this point. Malcolm also developed effeminate gestures and traits so that there would be no suggestion of masculinity which might cause him to get involved with his mother. His mother would not tolerate any masculinity or assertiveness on Malcolm's part, and mother and son gradually merged into a symbiotic, or mutually reinforcing relationship.

"I know this must make you sick," he said, testing my desire to help him. "You can't like me since I'm a homosexual."

"I told you, I'm interested in your self-destruction," I said. "I'm worried that you're going to hurt yourself."

I've never witnessed more intense anguish than in situations like the one in which Malcolm was trapped. He was looking for love, reaching out, becoming the little boy who wanted his mother to respond. But in seeking this love, he frequently got involved with rough, hostile homosexual men who abused him and then beat him up. Instead of being healed, he sank deeper into the morass of his emotional sickness. He wanted these other men to become his mother, but they brutalized him.

In the entire time that I counseled him, I never told Malcolm that his homosexuality was wrong. But as I emphasized that it was destructive, he came to understand that I thought it was wrong. He once challenged me by declaring, "I picked up a guy last night. You don't like that, do you?"

I didn't answer his question directly. Instead, I said, "Let's talk about what happened. Tell me about it."

After he described the incident, I said, "I think that subconsciously you still want to lose your job and your reputation. And you know why? Because somehow you think your mother disapproves of the success you're achieving. You're becoming independent, a person in your own right, and you don't need her any more. That makes you feel guilty because your mother has conditioned you to feel you always have to remain subordinate to her. You have to understand this deep need you have to destroy yourself, and learn to control it."

Healing had already begun by this point because he was transferring his feelings about his mother to me and expecting me to dominate, exploit, and emasculate him as she had done. If you find yourself in this position in your own counseling, you should be very sure that you've mastered any of your own unresolved homosexual feelings. Malcolm tested my sexual security by actually making a homosexual proposition. "You know, I wouldn't mind being with you," he said. "Want to try it?"

"Don't you have any idea what you're doing now?" I asked.

"What's that?"

"You're putting yourself in a position to be exploited. This kind of relationship is not a love relationship, it's mutual exploitation. It is no more loving than any other one-night sexual encounter. The basis of much homosexuality is hostility — hostility to a mother or to a parental situation that involved exploitation and a lack of love. You always take the passive role in these homosexual encounters, don't you? You always perform the fellatio. That's nothing but an infantile experience. You're re-creating your relationship with your mother by allowing yourself to be used."

It can be quite threatening for a latently homosexual therapist to be trying to help an overt homosexual and then find that the homosexual is making a pass at him. The tendency at this stage would be for the uncomfortable Christian counselor to say, "Okay, now you have to accept Jesus as your Lord and Saviour," and completely cut off any further emotional counseling. If that happens, the love linkage will end and any possibility for healing will be destroyed.

One of Malcolm's other personality problems was that, through his sick relationship with his mother, he had learned to kowtow to all authority figures in his life. If another teaching colleague said, "Run down and get me a sandwich," he'd go without question. In his own mind he was inferior to everyone else, even though he had many obviously superior intellectual abilities. I tackled this deficiency by using humor. One day, as he was leaving my office, I said, "By the way, Malcolm, on the way out would you clean my ash trays?"

His automatic reponse was, "Okay, sure," but then he saw I was grinning, and he asked, "Hey, what are you doing to me?"

I kidded him by saying, "I'm debating whether I should destroy a good thing by helping you overcome your problems. You know we need people like you to take care of the dirty work in this world."

He immediately got the point, which the smile on my face told him was the opposite of my words: I was really saying, "Malcolm, don't subject yourself to exploitation, because it's absurd. Be independent! Have some confidence. See yourself for the good, competent person that you really are!"

Malcolm finally began to accept himself as a worthwhile person who not only could, but *should* be free and independent of his mother's influence. His handwriting actually changed to a bolder, more masculine style during our sessions, and his voice deepened. Gradually, he lost his interest in having homosexual encounters and began to wonder what it would be like to go out with a girl. He knew where I stood on spiritual matters, and one day without any prodding on my part, he showed up for one of our sessions carrying a Bible. Taking this as an indication that the Spirit of God had begun to work in him, I answered some of the religious questions he had and encouraged him to find a church home. He's now an active charismatic Christian and is married to one of the young women he started dating during our therapy sessions.

Malcolm is a prime example of why I feel so strongly that homosexuals should not be abandoned to their frequently unhappy way of life. If professional psychotherapists, instead of bending to popular sociological theories and social movements, would just take an objective look at the patients who come in to see them, I think they would come to the same conclusion I have: Homosexuality is an emotional illness which can and should be cured through compassionate, loving therapy.

Malcolm, though, represents only one type of homosexual. Some men — the brutal sort who assumed the aggressive sexual role with Malcolm and then beat him up — have repressed their hostilities so deeply that they sometimes don't even regard themselves as homosexuals. A New Jersey detective named Mike came in to see me with a stomach problem. He had undergone numerous medical tests, and his doctors could find nothing wrong with him physically so they referred him to me. As Mike walked into my office and took a seat, I immediately got the impression that here was a man's man. He was tall, muscular, and very masculine and decisive in his bearing. But as he began to talk about himself in a tough voice, out of the side of his mouth, I saw that his machismo was laced with a substantial dose of cruelty.

"I haven't had to use my pistol for a whole year," he boasted. "I arrest guys with my fists. I've put twenty guys in the hospital — in critical condition — just since the first of this year.''

''What kinds of things do you do with your spare time?'' I asked.

''Bowling, drinking with the guys in local bars.''

''Do you get into fights much on your off hours?''

''Yeah,'' he said. ''I've decked a lot of guys in bars when I don't like their looks and they get smart with me.''

''Get smart?''

''Yeah, you know, I might sit down next to them at the bar and elbow them a little to get some extra room. Then the guy would say something, and I'm not about to put up with anything from some little squirt.''

''So you'd beat him up?''

''Yeah. I've had some real brawls, rolling around on the floor, but I haven't been beat up myself yet. The ones that really bug me are the little queers, though.''

''The queers?'' I asked, puzzled.

''Just the other night one of them came up to me and asked if I'd like to go out back with him and let him give me some fun. I said sure, and then I went out back and he did it and then, man, I let him have it — pow! right on the chin! I can't stand those dirty little guys. How can a man do something like that?"

"You mean how can a man perform a homosexual act?" I asked.

"Sure — I don't understand it."

"But who's really the homosexual?" I asked.

"What are you talking about?"

"You're performing a homosexual act too!" I declared.

For once, Mike had nothing to say. He stared at me with a look of shock in his eyes.

"I mean, it doesn't matter if you throw off on them and beat them up," I continued. "You've still performed a homosexual act yourself."

Mike now had lost his tough, masculine facade and looked as though he had fallen into a state of complete panic. "I sense a lot of hostility in you, and I think that may be the cause of your stomach aches," I said. "But the hostility is probably related to something that happened to you when you were much younger. Don't worry about those homosexual encounters right now. Just be honest with me and let's get to the bottom of this thing."

I discovered that Mike's family life in his Irish Catholic home had been quite complex and personally debilitating for him. His father had been an alcoholic who regularly abused and beat up his wife and children. The mother was so embroiled in her marital problems that she wasn't attentive to Mike, and he had a sense of being deprived of love. When his father hit him, he wanted to hit back, but he soon learned that opposition just enraged his father even more. Mike tried to release his rage against his mother, but that didn't work because she just acted hurt and made him feel guilty. She used a false kind of long-suffering attitude to exploit him and force him to obey her. Without an object for his anger, he learned to turn it back inside himself.

Mike's father died while he was in his early teens, but by then the damage had been done. In his dealings with people, Mike shifted back and forth from his father's brutalizing role to a role as the victimized young boy. Unsure of his own ability to be a real man, he decided to go into one of the most overtly masculine professions, the police department, to prove his manhood to himself. But underneath the machismo he exuded was a frightened little boy. If you took his gun or police shield away, he felt powerless. One of his main anxieties, he said, was that if the police learned he was in therapy they might put him on the "rubber gun squad." In that status, he could carry his gun but couldn't be issued bullets.

When Mike saw a small or effeminate man in one of the bars he frequented, he would subconsciously see a reflection of himself. He hated the weakling before him, assumed the role of his brutalizing father, and provoked a fight. When a homosexual approached him, something in Mike would respond because he desperately wanted love, which neither his mother nor his father had given him. But after the act of fellatio he realized this kind of love was counterfeit and, feeling guilty and humiliated, he resumed his dead father's stance of rage. He saw himself in the weak little homosexual and, unable to stand it, he had to lash out and destroy. In re-enacting these early family encounters, he was hoping to be healed, but he only succeeded in opening the old wounds and making the situation worse.

Mike covered up his homosexual tendencies, which he would not even admit to himself, by bragging at the station house about his conquests with women. ''I went out with this incredible broad last night, and I had to tell her I loved her to get her to do it for me,'' he said to one of his buddies. ''Man, was she surprised afterwards when I laughed at her!''

He did occasionally go out with prostitutes, but more often than not, he experienced some degree of impotence. Mike was stuck emotionally at a stage of adolescence, and the fact that he still saw his mother regularly didn't help matters. Neither his mother nor his father had helped him develop a strong, independent ego; so a sense of dependency drew him to his mother, and she continued to exploit him subtly and prevented him from expressing any anger toward her. He was making a good salary, for example, but he would regularly spend it all and then ask her for thirty or forty dollars at the end of the month. She would nag him at those times, but how can you get angry at an elderly lady who is giving you a substantial part of her small income? Her generosity was tinged with exploitation because she was lonely and knew she could use the money to control him if she played her cards right.

When I began to assume the Good Parent role in our sessions, I knew I was confronting a delicate, volatile situation. Mike was a very hostile, violent man, and if I pushed him too far, he might attack me physically. To protect myself, I always interviewed him when another man — my cousin Rudy or another analyst — was nearby. I think this sort of procedure would be advisable for you, too, if you're counseling a potentially violent person.

He expected verbal violence from me because his own father had treated him that way, and he tested me to see if I would react angrily. One of his ploys was to direct a stream of loud profanity toward me, and I finally allowed myself to get angry with him in a controlled way.

"Now look, Mike, I'm not going to stand for that," I said. "If you don't stop abusing me like that, then we'll just terminate the sessions."

He hadn't expected this response because all he had known from his father was physical violence. But now, in me, he had a father who was firm, but not brutal or abusive in retaliation. As he mulled over my words, I continued: "I want to work with you because I see some fine qualities in you. But there are certain things I won't put up with, and one of them is being degraded by having somebody shower me with curse words."

As I've mentioned in other contexts, a just, but well-managed expression of anger can be healthy in helping clear the air and providing opportunities for the person you're counseling to grow spiritually. The important restriction on displaying anger seems to be that we should use it sparingly, or be "slow to rouse your temper," as the

Scriptures say in several places (cf. Proverbs 15:18; James 1:19). Also, our anger should be resolved quickly and should not be allowed to turn into a grudge. The Apostle Paul wrote, *"Even if you are angry, you must not sin;* never let the sun set on your anger or else you will give the devil a foothold." (Ephesians 4:26 - 27).

I had another opportunity to display righteous anger toward Mike one day when my wife was standing out in the hallway with a patient. In an obvious effort to provoke me, he made some lewd remark about her, and I decided this had to be the showdown. "Okay, that's it!" I almost shouted. "You've gone too far now. We're through with each other. You'll have to find another therapist. Now get out of here!"

He immediately became very solicitous and begged me to forgive him. "Hey, I really didn't mean that," he said. "Look, I don't know why I say things like that — the thoughts just come into my mind, and I can't hold them back."

"Well, I've been trying to help you, but

I can't do it at the expense of the good reputation and integrity of my family members. That was a horrible thing to say about anybody, but about my wife, in my presence . . . I just don't know."

"Please, Dr. Calabrese!" he said. "I'm telling the truth. I didn't mean it. I'm really sorry, and it won't happen again. You've been great to me, and you're helping me, and I know it. I don't want to stop seeing you."

"All right, all right, let's forget it then," I replied after a brief pause. "But I really can't tolerate anything like that again, okay?"

"Okay," he replied, much subdued now.

Mike finally understood that he now had a father who didn't need obvious displays of machismo to assert his authority. He knew I wouldn't exploit him, yet he also knew I wouldn't be exploited myself. His improvement was marked after that incident. He stopped going to bars after work and began to do some normal, healthy dating. After going through a short, quite natural period of expressing anger toward his mother, Mike learned to control his temper with her. He finally began to understand her emotional problems and developed a sense of genuine filial love. There were no more homosexual encounters, and he eventually fell in love with a widow about his own age and married her.

Since I had become something of a model for him, he followed my example of attending Mass on Sundays, and to his surprise he found he enjoyed the experience. Mike's stomach problems are gone now, and he became active in establishing a Christian organization among the policemen in his New Jersey community. It was amazing to me how God's love and grace finally triumphed in his life because, instead of beating up criminals, he has now devoted his considerable physical energies toward reforming them. In our last session we actually prayed together. Mike's transformation was almost a textbook illustration of Paul's famous description of the Spirit-filled Christian life: "And for anyone who is in Christ, there is a new creation; the old creation has gone, and now the new one is here." (2 Corinthians 5:17).

Although male homosexuals usually remain that way unless therapy or some strong spiritual influence causes them to change, female homosexuals, or lesbians, frequently resolve their sexual problems while they're in their twenties and go on to lead normal, heterosexual lives in marriage. One young lesbian, Paula, failed to experience this natural change in her sexuality, and she came to me for help.

A Broadway actress, Paula was exceptionally attractive and talented, but she complained of severe depressions. She said she had gone through a period of promiscuity with men, but then had devoted herself to lesbian liaisons.

"I don't want you to analyze my homosexuality because I'm happy with that," she said. "I just want to get rid of these depressions."

"I'll deal with whatever sickness I see," I told her firmly. "I can't just separate one part of your personality from another part."

"Well, just don't you go analyzing it away," she said.

Promiscuity in both men and women is often related to homosexual tendencies because the latent homosexual is very insecure and has a constant need to prove himself sexually. He can't feel comfortable in just one heterosexual relationship. Paula had been a classic example of the connection between heterosexual promiscuity and homosexuality because, as a teen-ager, she got involved in affairs with several men in an effort to deny her homosexuality.

She was reared in a culturally Catholic home, but never learned to take her Christianity seriously. Her father was a heavy drinker who injected sexual overtones into his encounters with her. Her mother, a very weak woman, encouraged these unhealthy contacts between father and daughter by doing nothing to discourage them. I've actually known mothers who condoned incest by denying that it was happening: "Oh, that's just Daddy's way of showing affection," one woman insisted.

Paula's father sometimes came into her room late at night after a long drinking bout, sat down on her bed and hugged her, murmuring, "My little baby, my little baby." Paula, who was thirteen at the time, was no baby, and these incidents frightened her considerably. As we got further into our discussions, she admitted she had felt a tremendous degree of stimulation during these encounters. The only way she could defend herself was to deny her own sexuality. One method she used was to concentrate on the little girl's roles in school plays and later in professional productions. Paula refused to grow up because she was afraid of the feelings her father had encouraged. A woman's sexuality is often more dormant than a man's and needs to be awakened. Every girl wants a charming prince to kiss her and turn her into a real woman, but sometimes, as in Paula's case, the wrong person steps into the prince's shoes.

It's almost always a bad experience with the parent of the opposite sex that drives a child into homosexuality. If you're dealing with a homosexual and trying to determine the cause of the problem, concentrate first on his relationship with his mother if your friend is a male, or the father if she's female. Nudity among parents can have the same effect as the late night hugging of Paula by her father. One boy who was referred to me was almost driven into homosexuality because his voluptuous mother wandered around the house nude. The only way he could manage his sexual attraction toward her was to deny his masculinity.

In Paula's case, her father was negligent about covering himself up or closing the door when he was dressing or urinating. As a small child, she got frequent views of his sexual organs, which seemed exceptionally large since she was so small herself. When she learned what sex involved, she began to have nightmares about being ripped apart by a man during the act of intercourse. She denied these fears and the incestuous attraction she felt toward her father by denying that she was capable of being interested in any male.

Knowing her violent reaction to any moralizing about homosexuality I diligently avoided any references to the subject; instead, we taked about her "relationships."

"Tell me, Paula, what caused you to move from relations with men to relations with women?" I asked.

"I really had a thing for this good-looking, famous actor who was in the same show with me," she replied. "Well, I got him into bed with me, but it wasn't fun. He was so into himself, he didn't care whether I enjoyed the sex or not. The fantasy didn't live up to the reaity, and I figured, 'if this guy is inadequate, what man *can* satisfy me?' So I decided to try women, and that worked out a lot better."

"But you're still depressed," I reminded her.

"That's true, I am."

I explained to her that the depression resulted from several sources. She still harbored intense anger toward her father for putting her in situations that as a child she was incapable of handling effectively. She also was moving promiscuously from one lesbian encounter to another, just as she had behaved before with men. These superficial one-night stands were causing her to feel life was meaningless.

"You think each new sexual liaison will be the answer to your problem," I said. "But you're beginning to realize that's not the answer, and you don't know where to turn."

"As I worked with her to show how important it was to change her promiscuous tendencies, she started looking at me as the substitute for her father. But just like every other person I've counseled, she had to test me. She suspected the beneath my fatherly, spiritual facade, I was just like her real father.

"Hey, Doc, I've just moved into a new apartment," she said one day. "How about coming over to see it, maybe have a drink and give me some decorating suggestions?"

As she winked and smiled seductively, I knew she had more on her mind that room decoration. "I can't do it, Paula," I replied.

"Why not?"

"You may not even be aware of what you're doing, but you know you're sexually attractive. You know that many men in my position would be happy to have a good-looking actress on their arm. In the seclusion of your apartment, you'd like to see whether or not I can maintain this image I have now. Or would I become like your real father and make sexual overtures? I'm not going to get into that situation because I want to see you healed. I love you dearly — so much that I could never offer you a counterfeit kind of love which would be completely contrary to my own Christian values. I would have nothing to offer you if we got involved with each other, and I'd end up hurting, instead of helping you."

My discussions with Paula are another good example of the dangers that you may run into as you get into sexual counseling with a person of the opposite sex. Even if your friend is a homosexual, there is still a heterosexual potential lurking in her personality, especially if your therapy has been successful enough to help her cross the line back to a healthy orientation. I

282

can't emphasize strongly enough how important it is to be careful during this sensitive, fragile stage of your love treatment.

Paula eventually overcame her lesbianism and got married. Although she never really embraced Christianity, I'm satisfied that the seeds of Christian love were planted because she was sympathetic to the potential of the Christian faith when we parted ways. My dealings with such divergent personalities as Malcolm, Mike, and Paula have convinced me that homosexuality is curable and should be cured, not only because it's contrary to Christian morality but also because I've never known a practicing homosexual who had realized his full human potential. God's moral imperatives are not just a series of meaningless rules, but are rooted in the very structure and purpose of creation.

Chapter Ten

Creating a Conscience

Have you ever wondered why some people can cheat on their income tax returns or expense accounts and think nothing of it, while others are haunted by feelings of having done something wrong? Or why some people can ignore the fact that a restaurant waitress has made a mistake in their favor on a check, even though others feel a compulsion to set things straight?

These are minor examples of what we have come to know in popular terms as a "conscience" — or a consciousness of the moral rightness or wrongness of your acts. Your conscience is rooted in your superego, or your internal value system. The sensitivity of your conscience depends on how well your parents or other authority figures in your childhood impressed on you the properiety or impropriety of different kinds of conduct.

Some parents encourage the formation of *too* sensitive a conscience, and give their child standards that are more rigid than anything Christ ever demanded. We examined some examples of such oppressive value systems in Chapter Four and saw how the Christian love treatment can help you mold a more realistic superego. But at the other extreme, the parents who give their child no moral standards to follow are following an equally destructive path of child rearing. In the name of free choice they may refuse to teach any moral or religious standards. They say, "I don't bring my child up in any religion — he can decide later what he wants to believe." At age twelve or thirteen the boy or girl will probably decide to believe nothing. This approach represents an absurd extreme of our democratic assumptions about freedom and self-determination.

The three-year-old boy or girl has what amounts to a blank, or partially formed conscience or superego. He needs guidance from his parents, and if they don't provide it, his standards of conduct will develop at random. There will be no solid moral foundation for his personal value system, and the result for the child and for society at large will be anybody's guess, but you can expect the worst.

One set of parents who reaped the wild harvest of such permissive child rearing were beside themselves with worry when they brought their fifteen-year-old son into my office.

"He stays out all night, has had veneral disease, uses drugs — we don't know what to do with him!" his mother complained during an interview I had alone with her.

I agreed to work with the boy, whose name was Sheldon, but first I had to determine whether he was a complete sociopath. A sociopath is a person who has absolutely no sense of moral values. To this type of personality, stepping on a roach, sleeping with his best friend's wife, and killing a stranger on impulse have the same meaning. It's impossible for a sociopath to form any lasting relationship or friendship with another person. His lack of values prevents any bond of loyalty or love from forming, and his deficiency will always become evident as you try working with him. If you're dealing with a person who appears to have no superego at all, terminate the counseling session and insist that he seek professional help. A sociopath is by definition a psychotic or insane personality, and there is nothing a lay therapist can do to help him.

But if your friend or spouse can form a relationship with you, he has some superego, and you may be able to help. Sheldon immediately entered into a personal relationship with me. As he responded to my overtures of compassion and warmth, I knew he could improve with some effective counseling. The best approach to young man like this is to become a strong, authoritative father and heal his superego by helping him create a conscience.

My opportunity to assert moral authority over him came as he began to take more liberties with me in an effort to see how much he could get away with. Because his own parents had been quite permissive, he expected me to respond the same way. He started smoking in our sessions and flicked his ashes deliberately on my rug.

"I'd appreciate it if you'd use the ash tray, Sheldon," I said quietly, but he just smirked. He then put his feet, which were quite muddy, up on a couch which he knew I had just bought.

"Take your feet of that couch!" I said more sternly.

Defiantly, he tossed two words at me that the kids in my old neighborhood in Brooklyn used to write on the back of fences. With that, I released my reserves of righteous anger.

Storming out of my seat, I picked him up by the front of his shirt and shouted, "I've had it with you! Now get out of this office! I don't want to treat you!" and I shoved him toward the door.

I've never seen a young man look so shocked or become so pale in so short a time. A few minutes later, though, my telephone rang, and Sheldon was on the other end of the line. "Do you really mean it?" he asked in a subdued tone.

"Yes," I said. "I don't want anything to do with you."

"Look, I didn't mean it. Please take me back! I promise I won't do anything like that again. I'll do what you say."

"Well," I replied, "I can't put up with that sort of thing. I *won't* put up with it. You were showing no consideration for me whatsoever. But if you think . . ."

"Oh yes, I promise I won't act bad again."

"All right, if you promise . . . come on back and we'll finish your session."

When Sheldon provoked this incident, he wasn't fully aware of what he was doing. Subconsciously, he wanted to test me to see if I would be like his real parents, but then he became terrified when he realized he had caused me to reject him completely. About two years later, after his therapy sessions had finished, I ran into him in a store and asked how he was getting along.

He said he was doing well, and after we had talked for a few minutes, he asked, "You remember that time when you threw me out of your office?"

I laughed. "How could I forget it?"

"You know, that's the best thing you ever did for me."

Sheldon needed a firm hand to help him build a superego and conscience that would enable him to live a productive social life. Because I had assumed unequivocal parental authority over him, our relationship had been transformed, and the course of his life was changed. But sometimes this tough, physical approach to building an adequate superego is inappropriate, especially when you're dealing with a mature adult who might react to your forcefulness by injuring or even killing you.

A hardened criminal named Matt came to me with a severe stomach problem, and I immediately started worrying about my personal safety. Dressed like a typical gangster in an expensive, ostentatious silk suit and dark glasses, he began to pace up and down in front of me like a caged animal.

"Why don't you sit down?" I suggested.

"Yesterday, I was in a psychiatrist's office, and I almost threw him out of the

—— window because he ordered me to sit down," Matt growled.

Since we were on the twenty-second floor at the time, I decided not to puruse that line of conversation any further. But Matt continued: "I've killed eighteen people, and it didn't bother me one bit." He clapped his hands together. "It was just like that — just like killing a bunch of gnats."

By now, I was sure I had a full-blown sociopath on my hands, and I was really scared. It didn't seem possible to establish a relationship with a guy like him. He finally stopped his pacing, stretched out on a chair in front of me, and said, "Doc, I'm thirsty. Run out and get me a drink of water."

That did it. I couldn't take it any more. "The water fountain's outside," I replied. "You can get your own glass of water."

His upper lip curled slightly, and he said in a disturbingly calm voice, "I've killed guys for less than that."

"Look, you came to me for a problem with your stomach, right?"

"Yes."

"Well, if you frighten me, I won't be able to help you with your belly ache, and right now, I'm scared to death. There's only a fifty-fifty chance that I can help you anyhow. But there's *no* chance if we go on like this."

He sighed. "Okay, where's the water."

"Outside, around the corner," I replied.

From that moment, Matt and I began to develop a close personal bond, though I knew I could never shove him up against the wall as I'd done with the teen-ager Sheldon. Still, I had to assume the role of Matt's parent, so that I could help him develop some values and a good, solid conscience. The best threat of enforcement I had was to let him know I couldn't work with him if he didn't treat me properly.

Matt told me during our ensuing discussions that he had been given away five or six times by parents and guardians when he was a child. His mother put him in a Catholic home for orphans when he was quite young. The earliest recollection he had of solid authority figures were the priests in the home, who paced back and forth, saying the psalms in their breviary.

Seeing these strong-looking men walking around had given him some sense of security and comfort, but they didn't spend much time with him individually. The only thing his superego retained was the priests' walking, back and forth. When he didn't know what to do later in life, he would begin to pace, as he had done at the outset in my office, in the hope that the right course of action would be revealed to him.

After running away from this home a couple of years later, he bounced around, from one place to another. He never learned what set of values to follow, and he internalized the anxiety and rage that resulted from his state of uncertainty. His stomach problems were the final result. Matt's experience is common to many children who, even if they're not shuttled around, feel a lack of love and a lack of parental direction about what's right and wrong. All children crave this kind of moral guidance, even if they rebel against it. Parents who are too permissive are laying the groundwork for serious emotional problems during adolescence and adulthood.

As our relationship developed, Matt saw me as the Good Parent he had always wanted but had never found, and he actually began to love and even idolize me. The childlike allegiance he had given organized crime chieftains was now transferred to me. One day he brought in some expensive boating equipment which I had mentioned I was looking for.

"Where did you get that?" I asked.

"That's not important — I just want you to have it because you're a good friend," he replied.

"No, I don't want it because I know you stole it," I replied.

"So what if I did?" he said. "*You* didn't steal it, so it's all right for you to have it."

"No, it's not all right, because I can't go along with values like that. If I took that, I'd be condoning robbery and theft, benefiting from it, and I don't believe that's right."

We had several conversations like this, and gradually, I was able to re-educate him into accepting a healthier value system and to help him build up his superego. A father-son relationship developed between us, but I knew I had to be a stronger father than his underworld *capo,* so I began to plead and argue with him to reform. He started trying to extricate himself from his criminal connections, and a relative, who was a high-ranking mobster, finally interceded and got him out.

But even after Matt entered the legitimate business world, his journey to emotional health wasn't complete. "I've been having these terrible dreams, Doc," he said one day. "I keep seeing all the people I've murdered. It's like hell! I don't know if I can stand it."

"Let's examine those crimes a little more thoroughly," I said. "Why did you kill those people?"

"It was just a job to me at the time."

"That was before you had a conscience, right?"

"Yeah, but now I don't know if I can stand the guilt. They're no more, man, no more. They didn't do anything to me, but I just killed them like they were nothing."

I mentioned a few thoughts I had about God's willingness to forgive, but Matt wasn't ready for Christianity at that point. He finally learned to live with his guilt after he was arrested and convicted for a robbery he had committed before our therapy had begun. Almost relieved at the idea of going to jail, he said, "I did what they accused me of, and I know I have to pay for it. I'll come out and be able to live a better life."

The fact he had paid at least in part for his past crimes helped him to adjust to his new way of life. I believe that if he could also have accepted the fact that Jesus died as the ultimate payment for all his crimes and sins, his emotional healing would have occurred much faster. I don't know if Matt ever became a Christian because I lost touch with him after he was paroled. But I do know that God helped me to heal Matt's inadequate value system, which was destroying him and the people he was victimizing. This kind of healing is often a first step toward a meaningful faith in Christ.

There is at least one big qualification

you should keep in mind while you're trying to help your friend develop a stronger superego and a more sensitive conscience: Be sure that you don't make him depend on you too much as a parental substitute. Otherwise, his entire new value system — including any religious faith he may develop — may be tied up in his relationship with you. When he stops seeing you, his superego may crumble again. This kind of weak superego is one major cause of that great bane of Christianity — the backslide.

A young Christian man named Ted came to me with a marital problem, but I quickly saw that his difficulties went much deeper than his marriage. His mother and father had both held down jobs when he was a child, and they had been too exhausted when they got home to give him much guidance or surveillance. "I haven't got time for that now," his mother would say when Ted asked a question about cheating at school or whether Jesus was really God. "Let me rest up, and then we'll talk about it." But neither his mother or father ever seemed to get sufficient rest, and the topics were never discussed.

Because of this neglect, Ted developed a very weak superego, or internal value system, and he found himself always in a quandary about what was really right and wrong in different ethical situations. He eventually got married, but the marriage ran into trouble because he constantly abused his wife or cheated on her without really understanding that what he was doing was wrong. Ted finally came under the influence of a pastor, who began to fulfill the parental role that he had always wanted. As Ted incorporated this minister's value system, he found his own sense of right and wrong got sharper and his relationships with his wife and friends improved.

But then Ted became completely disillusioned when the pastor got involved with a woman. The affair caused a scandal in the church, the minister was fired, and Ted was left without a counselor. More than that, however, he was left without a superego, because the pastor had not encouraged him to think for himself and become independent. An unhealthy dependency had developed so that Ted felt he always had to run back to the minister for advice when a tough moral problem confronted him.

Ted's marital life soon reverted to an unhappy state, and he was back where he started, except that now he was oppressed by disillusionment. During our discussions, I told Ted, "Jesus Christ and your pastor merged in your mind. They became one and the same. But that's not true Christianity, not a healthy kind of faith. What you've got to do now is re-evaluate the values your pastor taught you and decide which part of this teaching was from Jesus, and which part from the minister. Your pastor became a parental substitute for you, and that's all right. But unfortunately, he didn't allow you to progress beyond the state of unquestioning childhood."

Ted was a backslider, but he hadn't fallen away from the faith because he wanted to. The mistakes his pastor made in counseling were as important a problem to overcome as Ted's unhealthy family background. Sometime a similar kind of backsliding, or falling away from Christianity, occurs when a young person has accepted his parents' faith without question and then finds himself on his own when he leaves for college or full-time work. His faith and value system are not his own and he finds himself "tossed one way and another and carried along with every wind of doctrine," as Paul puts it in Ephesians 4:14. In many cases of backsliding, the crucial mistake of the parent or counselor is to subordinate the personal power and presence of Christ to the personality of the adviser. If your friend's faith is in you, rather than in Christ, then his superego is just an extension of yours. He's probably destined for backsliding, rather than spiritual growth; for disillusionment and possible depression, rather than emotional healing.

Not all backsliding is related to weak conscience or superego, however. Perhaps the most common reason for veering away from a sanctified, Christ-centered life occurs when, as James put it, a person is ". . . seduced by his own wrong desire.

Then the desire conceives and gives birth to sin, and when sin is fully grown, it too has a child, and the child is death." (James 1:14 - 15). The psychological means through which our desires, or id-based animal instincts, work to seduce us into questionable or immoral actions is rationalization.

Chapter Eleven

Rationalization: the Backslider's Booby Trap

Some of the most bizarre excuses for gross immorality and inconsistent Christian living have echoed off the walls of my office that I can sometimes hardly believe my ears. The justifications range from "the devil made me do it" to outlandish arguments that would make even the devil want to avoid taking any credit.

The human mind is capable of almost any rationalization if that rationalization will induce some sense of comfort and moral consistency. Most of the time we rationalize when our animal, sensual instincts signal they want something badly, and our good judgment gives way to phony arguments that somehow manage to satisfy our conscience. In psychological terms, the desires of the id strike the ego, the center of our will and judgment, at a weak point. The ego then comes up with an excuse that momentarily quiets the warning signals from the superego. Sometimes our rationalizations are so clever that we can live for months or even years with the idea that we're morally consistent Christians. But God always puts the finger on the inconsistency, often through the words of another concerned Christian.

One church's religious education director told me her main problem was that she had lost a sense of her vocation. She didn't feel that she was doing God's work in the way He wanted her to, and she didn't know why.

"Have you discussed this matter with your pastor?" I asked.

"Oh yes, we see each other quite frequently. We have an especially deep relationship in the Holy Spirit."

Something in the tone of her voice made me suspicious so I asked her to explain what she meant. "Well, this may seem a little funny to you — it's hard to put into words," she continued. "But the pastor and I felt God leading us to deepen our relationship, so we've started seeing each other at a very tasteful, quiet hotel in a nearby town. He's not married of course — that would be quite wrong. But we know it's so right when we're together, alone in that room, just me and him and Him — the Holy Spirit. The Spirit's presence is so real when we touch each other. I . . ."

"Wait a minute, wait a minute," I interrupted. I couldn't take any more of this. "You were embracing each other under the Holy Spirit, is that right?"

"Yes."

"That's funny, because we used to call that something else in Brooklyn."

"You filthy pig!" she cried.

"Look, let's call it what it is," I said. "Let's be honest. I can tolerate it if you have sexual intercourse with this guy forty-five times this week, but I can't accept dishonesty. I can't help you if you're not going to be honest with me and with yourself."

It took her several minutes to calm

down, but I sensed that my straightforward approach had been necessary to impress on her what she was really doing with this pastor. It was important to strip away her rationalizations and bare the sordid facts about her fornication before any healing could take place. She had a very strict system of moral values and a strong sex drive, but her will power wasn't sufficient to balance the two without the help of rationalization. With the rationalization gone, our counseling relationship could begin in earnest. My first goal was to build up her weak ego, or will power, so that she could function as a more consistent Christian.

"Have you experienced any anxiety about your relationships with this pastor?" I asked.

"No, not until now," she said. "I just didn't feel quite effective about the church work I was doing."

"You're looking for something more substantial in life than this counterfeit relationship. Has this guy said he loves you?"

"Oh, yes."

"Is he going to marry you?"

"No, no. He has a single-minded dedication to his ministry, like the Apostle Paul."

"So what does he have to offer you in this relationship you have with him?"

"Trust and loyalty."

"To whom or what?" I asked. "He's not loyal to his ministry or to New Testament morality. He's not committed to you or the church if he's not willing to set this relationship of yours straight. You're looking for a good, loving companionship with someone, but you're settling for something that's false. You're forfeiting a beautiful love experience that you could have with someone else who is willing to dedicate himself to you as a husband. A man who really loves a woman wants to see her today and tomorrow and next year, on a full-time basis. You don't have that."

She finally overcame her tendency to rationalize, moved to another part of the country, and got involved in more meaningful Christian work. Her ego had been strengthened to the point that she could say, when another affair threatened to destroy her ministry, "I'm kidding myself — let's quit this." Almost all rationalization is a form of giving in to temptation. But if you can help a person heal his will power and strengthen his ability to exercise good judgment, the dangers of rationalization will no longer be so serious.

Another kind of rationalization that confronted me involved a pair of Sunday-school teachers who were carrying on an affair every Sunday morning before their classes. The young woman, Alice, was single, but Bob, her lover, was married. Although he regularly told his wife he had to leave early Sunday mornings for a little meditation before he taught his lesson, he actually spent the time contemplating his paramour. He came to me because he felt something was wrong with his marriage and he couldn't figure out what.

"Somehow, something seems to be lacking in my relationship with my wife," he said quite nonchalantly. Then he explained to me about the other woman, and concluded, "Of course, I know I'm saved. You can't lose your salvation. I believe God understands that I have this really strong sex drive and have to satisfy it somehow."

"I know a lot of people who have strong sex drives," I replied. "There's nothing so unusual about you except that you've convinced yourself that God tolerates what you're doing. I think we ought to take a closer look at this relationship you have with this girl. She's not married, right?"

"That's right."

"That means you're preventing her from getting married. You're keeping her from meeting another guy — in effect, abusing her through your rationalizations. How can God possibly be pleased with something like that? Paul said that by their fruits you shall know real Christians — what about these fruits of immorality you're bearing? Is it possible you're not in the Christian fold *at all* right at this point?"

With his defense of rationalization effectively destroyed, Bob was overwhelmed at first by regrets and guilt feelings. But as we got into his background, he began to understand why he treated women as objects to be used and then discarded. His mother had been unable to show him love, and he tried to get back at her by annihilating other females in cavalier sex encounters. He tried to tell me that he loved Alice deeply, but just as he was describing his devotion, another attractive woman walked by our open door and he whistled softly and said, "Wow!"

"I thought you loved Alice?" I said.

"I do," he replied.

"But you don't think love should involve any fidelity or commitment, is that it?"

Being well-versed in Christian morality, he immediately saw his inconsistency. As we aired all his rationalizations, and got to the core of the discrepancy between what he said he believed and what he did, his ego began to heal and be strengthened. Now Bob is a devoted family man who is much more active in Christian youth work. The energies that he dissipated in sexual escapades and the rationalizations he conjured up to rid himself of guilt feelings are now directed into more productive pursuits such as his business life.

Rationalization is a very common problem for all of us. Nobody has a perfect ego, and our judgment, will power, and personal identity are constantly changing. As the Apostle Paul says in Philippians 3:12: "Not that I have become perfect yet; I have not yet won, but I am still running, trying to capture the prize for which Christ Jesus captured me." Everyone at one time or another needs to have a Christian brother or sister point out the excuses he's using for inconsistent Christian living. That's one of the main ways we can grow.

It's extremely important to establish a love relationship with the inconsistent Christian you're counseling. Otherwise, you may become a condescending preacher and drive your friend into a defensive posture that will make it impossible to bring about any healing. People who have stumbled on the slippery slope of rationalization are in a very dangerous spiritual position. I've never known a truly committed Christian who could live in a constantly backslidden state. As Paul said in his letter to the Romans, "It is death to limit oneself to what is unspiritual; life and peace can only come with concern for the spiritual. That is because to limit oneself to what is unspiritual is to be at enmity with God: such a limitation never could and never does submit to God's law." (Romans 8:6 - 7).

Most rationalizers are well on their way to casting aside their Christian faith entirely. It's important to make them aware immediately of the direction in which they're headed, and help them scramble back to the firm ground of consistent Christian living.

Chapter Twelve

What Hath Our Culture Wrought?

Many of the emotional problems we've considered up to this point have had their roots in some unhealthy family relationship. But sometimes the primary blame for an inner wound must be laid at the doorstep of the culture in which we live. The most common environmentally induced psychological disturbances that are important for contemporary Christians to understand, afflict three main categories of people — women, blacks, and members of closed, oppressive churches. As we examine each of these groups in turn, decide how you may be able to help your own friends and relatives who suffer from similar difficulties.

1. Women in crisis. The contemporary feminist movement has done a great deal for women in the business world. There is more pressure on employers to give all their employees, both male and female, equal pay for equal work. A woman's innate talents and abilities are more likely to be recognized now than they were a few years ago. But along with the benefits of the women's rights movement, there have been detrimental effects.

There is a tendency in a democratic society, which we have mentioned before, to carry our egalitarian principles to an extreme and regard everyone as not only equal politically, but also the same in every other way. Any intelligent person with a modicum of common sense should be able to see that women are not the same as men. There are basic physical and psychological differences, but some radical feminists are not willing to recognize these differences and here is where the emotional problems begin.

Victoria, an executive secreary for a large corporation, complained to me about some problems she was having with her young son and husband. "My husband is always bothering me one way or another — he just uses me sexually and forgets I have rights too," she said. "And the kid — he's always whining, refuses to do what I tell him to do, won't behave around our baby sitters."

"You leave him at home during the day with baby sitters while you're working?" I asked.

"Yes."

"Well, it seems to me you have a great responsibility for that child. He's showing certain insecurities — probably because you're not around to mother him. He didn't ask to be born, but he has a right to a mother. Instead, you're in effect giving him two working fathers who are too tired to act as real parents."

"What century are you living in?" she cried. "You're a male chauvinist pig if I ever saw one."

"You can call me whatever names you like, but I won't respond to that sort of thing," I replied. "You're sitting across from my desk now because your marriage is about to break up and your child is in trouble. Your baby sitters are complaining about his aggressive behavior. Damage has already been done. But you go ahead and call me what you want and get it out of your system."

"Maybe you don't understand what's been happening in this country lately!" she protested. "Women aren't slaves any more! They have rights!" At that, she pulled a brassiere out of her pocketbook and said, "Look at this! I don't wear bras any more — I refuse to wear them!"

"But you still carry them around in your purse so you can show them off," I said. "Well, not in a million years will I take off my jock and wave it at you."

She laughed at that and relaxed a little. The thick cloud of feminist rhetoric seemed to have dissipated, so I started encouraging her to tell me about her relationships with her parents. Her reaction to me, I suspected, was related to a problem with her father, and perhaps her mother. She was skeptical of my approach at first. *"Society* — not my parents — made me and other women the way we are," she said.

"That's like saying the devil made you do it," I responded. "It's not just society, or the devil either. You have some individual responsibility, and you can change your life if you want to."

As she talked about her parental relationships, I immediately detected a strong hostility toward an overbearing father. "He abused me and my mother," she said. "He sometimes hit my mother, and there was nothing I could do about it. I'll have to admit, sometimes I hated him."

"Did you ever consider that your mother may have been a little masochistic herself?"

"What do you mean?"

"I mean she probably *needed* the abuse your father dished out," I explained. "That's the reason she married him. The victim may seek out the murderer, in a sense. If she had really wanted to change things she could have ordered him out of the house, or gone to a lawyer or a pastor, or just left him. But she saw herself as victim and apparently, down deep inside, had some need to play the role."

Victoria sniffed. "Frankly, I'm finding *all* men that way. They like to humiliate women, use them as sex objects."

"I know that's your attitude," I replied, "and that's the role you're assuming with your husband. You're *expecting* him to be abusive, just as your father was. And your feminist convictions are reinforcing this need you have to lash out and fight your husband, as though he were your father. If he makes a normal sexual overture to you, you interpret that as sexual exploitation or abuse. You've apparently decided, perhaps subconsciously, that the only way you can assert your rights as a woman is to become a man. So you're trying to become your father in your relationship with your husband. And it's tearing your family apart, isn't it?"

She was silent for a moment, and then nodded.

During our subsequent sessions, she transferred her feelings about men to me and occasionally tried to interpret some of my actions as attempts to abuse her. When I made a legitimate demand that she arrive at our sessions on time, she said,

"You just think you're so superior as an analyst here. And you think I'm nothing, don't you? Well, I won't be put down."

By the time I had convinced her that punctuality had nothing to do with male chauvinism, but was just an essential feature in a well-run office, she was off on another track: She failed to pay for a couple of sessions, and when I reminded her, she retorted, "You're always asking me to give you money. I saw that new car outside. I bet you bought it with the money I gave you."

"You haven't *given* me anything," I said. "I *earned* it. If I had to rely on your fees to buy a car, I wouldn't have one."

We had many stormy sessions before Victoria finally realized I was interested in her as a person and not as a feminist adversary. She finally decided to quit her job and devote more time to her son until his psychological problems were straightened out. But she continued to pursue her career objectives by returning to college part-time to take some business courses. By the time her child entered school, she had a degree in business

318

administration and was hired for a managerial job that paid more and involved more responsibility than her old secretarial position.

Victoria, like many other young women in our society, was in effect pushed through a second identity crisis because of the pressures she felt from the feminist movement. She had, in one sense, remained an adolescent bride for several years, until the women's movement awakened her to other talents she possessed, and that was a good thing. But she decided that home life would not ultimately fulfill her, so a career of some sort became a necessity. The danger with the feminist movement's influence is that some women, like Victoria, go to an extreme and abandon any sense of responsibility to their husbands and their children. A Christian approach to human relationships involves taking these responsibilities quite seriously because the happiness of a family and the personality development of the children hangs in the balance.

My experience in counseling people with a variety of emotional problems has convinced me that it's important for a loving mother to be available during the first years of a child's development. Although I would suggest that you give the same advice to women who come to you for help with their identity problems, stressing the importance of motherhood doesn't mean asking a woman to forget her career ambitions. I would only recommend accommodating those ambitions to the needs of the home and children, especially when the kids are in their impressionable preschool stage of development.

2. *The black man's burden.* A blond, blue-eyed female social worker ran into my office one day and said, "There's a patient waiting outside for help, but I can't counsel him! He's a big, black, sexy guy, and I just don't think it would be appropriate for me to get into any intimate discussion with him."

I went out to the waiting room, and the only person I saw there was a very unhappy-looking, average-sized, middle-aged black man. I asked him to come into my office, and learned that he was an unemployed father of several kids who was quite depressed because he had just lost his job. He was anything but sexy, as far as I could see, but this young woman's culturally induced anxiety had intensified when she saw him. She found herself unable to treat him as just another human being.

Many white people in our culture repress their own animal, id-based instincts, but then project all these sensual impulses onto the nearest black man. The black becomes a thinly disguised sex maniac, an uninhibited libidinal force that we have to control by social and political discrimination and prejudice. Some whites dream about blacks, who become symbols of strong, subconscious sexual feelings.

Ironically, the opposite is also true. Blacks sometimes dream about whites who become the black man's representative of unbridled sexuality. But the black faces a particularly serious emotional challenge because white attitudes put pressure on blacks to perform sexually, athletically, and in other overtly physical ways. In his anxiety to live up to these expectations, the black man may find that he has become impotent. In dealing with blacks who face emotional problems, you'll find it necessary not only to understand their relationships with their parents, but also how they react to the hostile white culture around them.

Charles, a well-educated black man in his mid-thirties, came to me because he was having problems with his wife. He had gotten involved with a couple of other women even though his wife was quite warm and beautiful, but he found he suffered periodic impotency when he tried to have sexual relations. Also, he couldn't pass his exams to become a Certified Public Accountant, even though he had plenty of native intelligence.

"Man, nothin's goin' right, man," he said with a thick ghetto accent that somehow seemed incongruous with his graduate school education.

He told me his mother had been the strong parent in the family. His father had trouble holding down a job and was constantly downgraded by whites by being called "boy" and other condescending terms. Charles's earliest memories of his father were of a person who was a failure, powerless in the presence of his wife or authoritative white figures. After he got married, Charles found his wife was becoming more and more like his mother — the main breadwinner while he was in school and the one to whom the children always seemed to turn for comfort and advice. He knew part of the problem was in himself, but he didn't know how to assert himself effectively except by shouting or an occasional slap. It was obvious to me that he was sinking steadily into the role he had seen his father take because he didn't know how a black man could act otherwise.

One day when he entered my office, his black ghetto style was even more pronounced than usual: "Hey, man, whatcha doin'?" he mouthed almost unintelligibly as he slumped down in his chair. He then pulled out a long nail file and began to pick his fingernails and stare at me insolently.

The time had come, I decided, to force

the issue: "You graduated from a good university, didn't you, Charles?" I asked.

"Yeah."

"You studied literature, went to graduate business school, yet here you are talking like a guy who never went to school at all. You're waving that nail file around at me, trying to communicate terror because you think that's the way niggers should act around white men."

His eyes widened, his mouth fixed in anger, and he jumped up with his fists clenched. For a moment I thought he was going to lunge at me. "Maybe you'd better explain yourself," he finally growled.

"Sure. How long are you going to try to get me to treat you like a nigger, and how long are you going to act like a nigger?" When I say 'nigger,' I don't mean a *real* black man — I'm talking about the *stereotype* of the black man that white society has imposed on you. You've given up, Charles! You've achieved, progressed, improved yourself in so many respects, but now you're reverting to that old nigger stereotype."

He sat down and nodded his head. "I don't like that word — nigger. At least not the way I thought you were using it. But you're right. I guess I am giving up and falling back into the old stereotype."

"And it's an *impotent* stereotype," I said. "White society has kept your father powerless, and you feel the same thing happening to you. It's destroyed your confidence to be able to perform on this professional exam, which is a mark of achievement in white society. And it's made you unable to perform properly in bed. You're going to have to learn to overcome the sense of inevitable defeat you feel when you come into contact with white society."

"That's easy for you to say because you're white and I'm black!" he said.

"Thanks for reminding me because I have a tendency to forget we're different colors," I said, and he chuckled. "I relate to you as Charles, not as a black man."

From then on I became not just a Good Parent for Charles, but also a *good representative of white society*. He had to straighten out the problems his mother and father had imposed on him, but even more important, he had to learn to relate to white people with confidence, on a level of equality. As he realized that I accepted him and thought highly of his abilities, his sex life began to improve and he became a better husband. He also passed his CPA exam and launched a promising career with a big accounting firm. Even though he had been quite active in Christian work as a youngster, he had reacted against the church because, he said, "the church keeps the black man down. Jesus was a white man."

Rather than allow a religious argument to develop, I used humor to show him where he was wrong: "We don't really know whether Jesus was a white man or not," I said. "But we do know he wasn't an Italian, and how do you think that makes me feel? I'd really prefer that He had come from Italy."

Charles had made no firm Christian commitment when I stopped seeing him, but his debilitating alienation from white society had been healed and he was leading a productive life.

The situation of blacks in our society has improved during the past few years, partly because militant organizations have helped blacks overcome the feelings that white society has castrated them. It's a shame that we as Christian haven't taken the initiative and stepped into the vacuum that the militant political organizations have filled. The Black Muslims, Black Panthers, and other groups have given the black a sense that he can achieve and control the world around him. But too often white Christians have encouraged segregated church congregations and subordinate or nonexistent roles for blacks in church hierarchies. The black man has the potential in the Christian faith to be proud of his identity and confident that God will help him realize his full spiritual and occupational destiny. Unfortunately, white Christians have too often fallen short by not making blacks feel accepted as fully equal believers. The time has come for us to assume the role of the Good White as well as the Good Parent in therapeutic personal relationships with our black brothers and sisters.

3. Are you strangling on your church's apron strings? A Spirit-filled church congregation should be a kind of Good Parent for individual members with emotional problems. Those with inner wounds should find themselves accepted and comforted by the church, just as their real mothers did or should have done when they were children. Sometimes, though, a local church will become the insensitive, unloving, oppressive mother, and believers will literally find themselves strangling, emotionally, on their church's apron strings.

Arnie, a man in his early thirties who was a member of a very conservative congregation with Old World roots, experienced a terrible personal tragedy just when life seemed about to reward him with great success and happiness. His young wife, a vibrant, committed Christian, contracted a terminal illness and died, leaving him with several small children. He had always been a devoted, faithful husband, and was so grief-stricken that he was afraid he might not be able to continue functioning as a father and successful businessman.

His church members gave him some moral support, but he found the greatest comfort in the companionship of a young widow, who was also a member of his congregation. An honorable and morally upright man, he refused even to consider moving in with this woman and conducted their relationship in a completely open, above-board way, in full view of the other church members. But the church leaders wouldn't have it.

"Your wife has only been dead a couple of months," one of the laymen chided him. "It's not appropriate, not right, for you to be dating her so soon."

"We haven't done anything wrong," Arnie replied. "You've seen us together in the church services. She just holds my arm, that's all. I'm affectionate toward her kids and she's great with mine, and that's it."

"I don't care," the man said. "It doesn't look right, and several people are saying you two have started an immoral relationship. We can't have that. We should avoid even the appearance of immorality."

"But that's just gossip!" the young man protested. "And anybody who thinks that it appears to be immoral for an unmarried man and woman to see each other in church, has to have a distorted mind."

But the lay leader wouldn't listen to this argument, and he told Arnie that if the relationship continued, the couple would have to leave the church. Arnie's family had been going to this church for years and he wanted to remain a member, so he decided to try to eliminate the problem by proposing to the young woman. She accepted, but when they announced their engagement, one of the older women who had opposed their relationship from the beginning, pulled him aside and said, "It's indecent, to behave this way only three months after your wife's death! We won't permit this! You won't be married in this church, if I have anything to say about it!"

Sure enough, the opposition was sufficiently vocal to intimidate the pastor, and he refused to perform the ceremony.

The couple was asked to leave the church and Arnie complied, but still felt torn between his loyalty to his fiancee and his congregation. Finally he came to me for advice.

"I want to marry her, but at the same time I don't think I can stand to cut my ties with the church," he said.

"Why?" I asked. "I don't understand why you want to stay at that place."

"The people there have always been so good to me and my relatives. I grew up there. It's like cutting ties with my own family."

"But look at what those people are doing to you," I said. "You could have a secret affair with this woman, and as long as you weren't open about it, even if they suspected what was going on, you'd be accepted by them."

"That's probably true," he said.

"Look objectively at what's happening," I continued. "Here you are, a young man whose wife has been dead for a few months. You're going out with a woman you want to marry, and you're being punished for that. I find nothing in the

Scriptures or in legitimate church tradition to support such a ridiculous notion. What I want to do now is examine why you feel such a strong desire to stay in that church when you're being abused like this."

As we explored his family background, I found that what amounted to an extended family situation had developed in that congregation. The life of Arnie's family had actually been tied up in the congregation for several generations, ever since the church members had immigrated *en masse* to the United States a century before. Older church members felt free to discipline younger people in the congregation who were not their own children. A very rigid, un-Christian kind of morality had grown up in this inbred religious community, and the pressures on the younger church members to conform were enormous. The definition of sin had become so broad that a person couldn't enjoy life without transgressing some rule or precept.

"What's happened is that your church has in effect become your mother," I told him.

"What do you mean?"

"As a child, with the encouragement of your parents, you transferred many of your normal feelings of respect for authority from them to your church. The problem is that this church, with the broad power it exercises over so many people, has a lot more power than your parents could ever have. You've moved away from your parents, but you can't seem to move away from your church. In many ways, you've remained an immature child, always seeking advice and instruction from church elders."

"So what can I do about it?"

"It's obvious, isn't it?" I said. "You moved away from your real parents, so isn't it logical to assume you can also move away from the influence of this substitute parent, the church?"

"You mean give up my faith?"

"Hardly," I replied patiently. "I mean, doesn't it seem clear that what these people are doing to you and other young people is wrong, even crazy? Now if you had a nutty mother who was oppressing you, keeping you from leading a free, independent spiritual life, it would be advisable for you to move out of her home. Well, in effect you *have* got a crazy mother — this church — and the best thing you can do is move away. Find another place of worship and live with *God* as your ultimate guide, not these authoritarian church elders."

Arnie finally did move away, found another church home and married his fiancee. He then began to build a normal life as a spiritually mature adult. His experience, you might argue, is unusual and extreme, but others have also been exposed to distorted views on sex and marriage under the cover of pseudo-Christian authority. As we've seen, there are many such cultural pressures that may affect an individual's emotional health, and when you're counseling a friend, you must always be alert to this possibility. If you're a man counseling a woman, she may see you as a representative of the male oppressors. If you're a white counseling a black, you may be regarded not as an individual human being, but as a symbol of the "honkie power structure."

In these situations, which may involve any socially or politically sensitive minority or interest group, you must establish yourself as a concerned, loving human being before the Holy Spirit can work and heal through you.

Even if a person's family or work life is free of these special cultural problems, there is a more general sort of social phenomenon that can block effective performance on the job and in recreation. Our society has fostered an insidious attitude which prevents many people from reaching their full potential or from enjoying achievement if they do succeed. I'm referring to an unhealthy sense of competition. It's one thing to want to do your best and come in first, but something entirely different to have an inner need to completely conquer or even destroy an opponent.

Chapter Thirteen

Healthy Competition or Symbolic Murder?

An elderly minister I know was called out of town and asked the pastor of a nearby church to fill in for him at a church service. During his substitute sermon, however, the visiting cleric said, "I have some doubts about whether you've really been hearing the gospel here. I'd suggest you try my church next Sunday if you want some more stimulating teaching and preaching."

When the older pastor returned and heard these comments he was furious. He called up the younger minister and said, "Listen friend, the Bible says feed my sheep, not steal them."

After learning of this incident, I realized that even the church sanctuary is not immune to the destructive effects of uncontrolled competitiveness. Competition can be a very good thing; it's essential for the improvement of business services and products and the development of personal skills. But sometimes competition becomes a kind of symbolic or ritual murder, which involves the destruction of the opponent's character and self-esteem. An overly ambitious person can never really win. He may score more points in a game or make a little more money than the business down the street. But the exhilaration of the conquest quickly evaporates, and it's necessary to seek out other adversaries and win again and again, with no hope of lasting satisfaction in the victory. The personality conflicts that arise in such competition result in alienation and antagonisms that may never be resolved.

Most people who are attracted to this vicious kind of rivalry believe they are worthless. They have to win in order to feel equal to other human beings. But as they alienate people and make enemy after enemy, they reinforce the idea that others don't accept them. These feelings of inferiority often stem from the influence of parents who never praised them when they achieved some honor as youngsters. Some people I've known had parents who criticized them for making a B+ on their report cards; but when they finally earned an A, the mother or father just said, "Well, we expected that."

A businessman named Alfred came to me for help because he had been a member of two tennis clubs, and top players in both had avoided playing with him. The reason, he said, was "they felt I was too competitive."

"What's the matter with those guys?" he asked me. "Are they afraid of a little tough game every now and then?"

"Well, obviously you feel there must be something wrong with *your* attitude or you wouldn't have come to see me," I said. "Now why don't you give me some of the details about these games you play with these fellows."

With considerable prodding on my part, he admitted that he often mixed in dead balls when he was serving and heckled the players on the other side to make them lose concentration. This poor sportsmanship was also evident in his business dealings. As a manufacturer of ball-point pens, he frequently told lies about his competitors in an effort to get their clients to switch their business to him. Alfred had become moderately successful with these underhanded tricks, but he was also a hated man who had been blackballed from the social gatherings of others in the field.

"But I don't really care about that," he said. "The thing that really gives me a kick is to see how many of those other guys I can drive out of business."

Alfred's background was typical for such a hard-nosed competitor. He had been adopted, and his mother told him several times, "You should be grateful to us, because nobody else would have taken you into their family." This attitude was in sharp contrast to a little boy I worked with, who was so proud he was adopted that he said, "I'm special because my parents picked me out of all those other kids."

Alfred's mother constantly made him

feel like dirt, and his father, a ruthless businessman, gave him an excessively aggressive model to follow. Alfred saw that his father was successful, so he decided if he also worked hard and stepped on other people, he would be able to show his parents that he really was worthwhile. This perverted kind of achievement orientation drove Alfred to unprincipled competition in everything he did. He learned to cheat in school because he felt the good grades were more important than the methods he used to get them. When he grew up and got into business, he ran roughshod over people to build up his enterprises. But when he got into a genteel athletic club, the heavy-handed tactics he had used in the marketplace didn't go over too well.

"I started working my way up on the tennis ladder, but after I'd moved about halfway up, suddenly I couldn't get anyone to play me any more," he said. "They were polite but they always had some excuse. I'll admit I occasionally called balls out that weren't actually out, but my opponents didn't make an issue of it. Why didn't they challenge me if they were upset? They should have cleared the air, rather than just excluding me."

"From what you've told me, your cheating at tennis is just an extension of the way you've competed in every other aspect of your life," I observed.

"I guess it is."

"And in every other case you've alienated people, so why do you expect things to be different on the tennis court? The problem is that you haven't minded making enemies in business, but you can't afford to make enemies if you want to play tennis regularly. That's a leisure activity that most people want to be fun and recreational. They don't want to have their characters assassinated every time they play. With your attitude toward competition, you can't expect to get people to associate with you socially. And tell me something honestly: Do you really enjoy these little temporary killings — and I mean character killings — that you make in business?"

He thought for a moment and said, "Well, I get a kick out of winning a big contract. But I don't enjoy the day-to-day work because the people I deal with are obnoxious and hard to work with."

"Maybe that's because *you're* a very intelligent, experienced, and energetic guy. Just the sort of person who could really go to the top in your field if you took a healthier approach to competition."

"What do you mean?" he asked, interested in anything that would help him improve his business position.

I explained to him how his unhealthy competitiveness resulted from his relationship with his parents, and told him that if he could learn to work with others in the field, rather than symbolically killing them, he would probably improve his sales by leaps and bounds. Not only that, he'd have a much better chance of getting some matches with the club's best tennis players.

"Really, you're killing yourself more than your competitors," I said. "You're keeping yourself from reaching your full potential in business, tennis, and everything else because you can't engage in a healthy, constructive kind of rivalry. You don't have to demolish other people to prove to yourself you're worthwhile. Just take an objective look at yourself, and you'll see how many talents and good qualities you have. Your mother was dead wrong when she failed to praise you for the good things you accomplished as a child.''

As Alfred's supportive friend, I built up his ego and helped him to like himself more and be satisfied with what he was capable of achieving. It took him a while to convince his business competitors that he wasn't pulling some dirty trick on them when he tried to be friendly, but after a few months of effort, he succeeded. He also started playing a less vicious brand of tennis, and some of his club's top players began to call him up for matches because they knew they'd get a game which could end with a genuine handshake.

If Christians could convince more people in this world to be eliminate their unpleasant, stressful killer instinct in competition, we might encourage an environment in which social harmony and love would become more important values. And when people begin to value love, they inevitably must consider the ultimate example of love, Jesus of Nazareth. As Christ becomes the motivating force in our lives, we can say, with the Apostle Paul, "Whatever your work is, put your heart into it as if it were for the Lord and not for men." (Colossians 3:23). With a Spirit-centered approach to achievement, competition becomes not ritual murder, but a creative encounter in which we do our best and try to win, but also have the potential of enchancing personal relationships with our competitors.

Chapter Fourteen

Home Remedies for Bad Habits

Everyone I know, including myself, has some bad habit — laziness, overeating, nail biting, bad hygiene — which may not seem particularly serious, but which can hinder our ability to relate to others. As a Christian, you have a responsibility to help your spouse or friend overcome these bad habits if they get too serious. But you may find yourself facing a painful, thankless task because usually those with bad habits are unaware of the effect they're having on others. They may believe they don't really have a problem, and won't bother to come to you for help. You'll have to take the initiative and that takes courage.

A friend of mine named Bob found

himself getting some unsolicited advice when he was serving in the military. He was sitting in the bachelor officer's quarters with an army buddy after a hard days work and he decided to take his shoes off and prop his feet up on a hassock in front of a fan.

After they had sat and talked for a few seconds, Bob's friend looked at him seriously and said, "You know, Bob, we've been friends a long time, haven't we?"

"Sure," Bob replied, with a questioning look on his face. "Why?"

"Do you mind if I say something very personal to you? As a friend, I feel as though I should — for your own good."

"Sure, go ahead," Bob said.

"You have the worst smelling feet I've ever come across."

Bob was embarrassed, and quickly put his shoes back on. But in the long run he appreciated his friend's advice and made it a point to change his socks more regularly and use foot powder. If his friend hadn't been willing to point out this personal deficiency, Bob might have driven away people who didn't know him well enough to criticize him. As Christians, we should follow the guidelines set down by the Apostle Paul: "If we live by the truth and in love, we shall grow in all ways into Christ, who is the head by whom the whole body is fitted and joined together." (Ephesians 4:15). Living by the truth in love — that takes courage, and exposes us to rejection. But being straightforward and honest in a genuinely concerned and helpful way is one of our responsibilities in our personal encounters. And there's no better remedy for bad habits.

When you're trying to help someone beat a bad habit, the general approach to the problem is the same as for any other emotional disturbance: try to understand why he behaves as he does, get him to trust you as a substitute parent or trusted adviser, and begin the process of re-education. No matter how diplomatic and sensitive you are, though, not everyone will be as receptive to criticism as my friend with the smelly feet. You are bound to hurt some feelings, so be prepared for defensive counterattacks. For example, a woman who came in to see me about another problem, had done well in overcoming many of her emotional problems, but she had never learned the importance of using a deodorant to kill underarm body odor. She had gained a great deal of confidence in her ability to succeed in the job market and came into my office one day dressed to kill. She said she had a job interview and was sure she would be hired.

"You'll probably never get that job," I said.

"What do you mean?" she asked, her enthusiasm now deflated.

"You have a very strong body odor. I smelled it when you came through the door."

Her face flushed and she cried "I hate you! I hate you!" and she ran out of the office.

I tried to stop her, but she wouldn't listen, and I was sure I had lost her for good. But the next day she called me up and said, "I got the job."

"Great!" I said, relieved.

"And I wanted you to know I showered

and used a deodorant before I went in for the interview. I'm sorry for the way I acted, and I'll never forget what you did for me yesterday. After I calmed down I realized how concerned you are about me and how really difficult it must have been for you to tell me that. You knew it would hurt me at first, and there was a chance I'd reject you entirely."

This woman had grown up in a home where the parents ignored personal hygiene, and she got so used to offensive odors that she was unaware when her own smells were alienating those around her. Because I had overcome my natural reluctance to criticize her, she now had embarked on a re-educative process to learn how to make herself more attractive and acceptable to others.

Of course, it's important to pick the right occasion to speak "the truth in love." Your friend should be in a position to take some time to discuss the matter with you if he wants. And by all means, make sure you mention his bad habit in private, not in a group where he may be embarrassed. In one large dinner party, one man said in a loud voice to an acquaintance at the other end of the table, "You know, Mark, your breath really smells lousy tonight. When you leaned across to talk to me on the sofa, I thought I'd choke."

It takes an extremely secure person to shrug off a comment like that and turn it into a joke. And the motivation of the person giving the "advice" has to involve some unresolved hostility — perhaps a desire to retaliate in a childish way for some imagined wrong.

There are many other bad habits that can be attacked with these techniques, but some problems may have roots that go much deeper than superficial personality defects. Overeating, for example, may be simply the result of excessive fondness for sweets, and an exercise of the will power may be sufficient to resolve the problem. But obesity can also stem from a sense of being deprived of gratification in human relationships and a need to build up a defense — a load of fat — against people. Compulsive eaters were often deprived in some way at their oral stage of development, when the child concentrates on putting things into his mouth. Perhaps their mother gave them spoiled food, or let them go hungry for too long on a consistent basis. In an attempt to heal this sense of deprivation these people eat constantly; they *destroy* food as a way of releasing their frustrations at being unable to find sufficient gratification in professional and personal encounters.

Because obesity may involve a serious personality problem, I'm always cautious in dealing with the eating habits of fat people. I don't attack the person's waist line directly, or risk insulting him in some way. Fat may be a defense against an underlying psychosis, or insanity. If a fat person goes on a crash diet and loses all his excess poundage, he may find himself defenseless against the world and be unable to cope. The first thing for you to do as a concerned Christian friend is to show love and help him heal his underlying emotional problem. As this problem is resolved and your friend gets a better image of himself, the fat will begin to come off naturally.

Habitual lying, like overeating, may also be either just a bad habit or a sign of a much more serious mental problem. Some inveterate liars who actually believe their fantasies are true, may be victims of schizophrenia, a psychotic condition that involves a disintegration of the personality and usually requires hospitalization or drug treatment. If you encounter someone you suspect is in this category, guide him immediately to a professional therapist. On the other hand, the tall-story teller who knows he's fibbing but just likes to embellish his conversations is in less serious condition, and you may be able to help him overcome his problem.

Usually, these neurotic, as opposed to psychotic, liars have a weak ego — a sense that nothing they do is itself worthwhile. Each of their experiences has to be embellished by fantasy to make it acceptable to others. One man who came to see me about another problem turned out to be a compulsive liar because his parents had not shown him enough love or approval when he was young. It took several sessions for him to let down his guard with me, but he finally admitted, "I'm never really happy, even when I get a promotion or receive a compliment on something I've done. I always feel as though it's not quite enough, like maybe I really don't deserve it."

Because life was never quite tolerable for him, he always improved upon his actual experiences in conversations, and the fibs made him feel better temporarily. He lied to me on several occasions during our conversations, but I learned to rely on my intuition and challenge him when I thought he wasn't telling the truth. I soon learned that the body language he used — an unusually direct stare or a certain set to his mouth — indicated that a lie was in the making.

As I built up his ego and pointed out the many strengths and talents I saw in him, the need to lie eventually diminished. I've had many such individuals who have worked out beautifully in treatment.

A question that may still be bothering you, especially with respect to obese people and habitual liars, may be, "How can I be sure that these people just have bad habits and are not suffering from a psychosis are requires professional treatment?'' The guideline that I would suggest is rather simple: when you're in doubt, insist that your spouse or friend seek out professional help. But before we leave this subject, let's take a closer look at some of the characteristics of the psychotic, or seriously insane, mind.

Chapter Fifteen

A Word of Warning About Psychotics

I was walking down Fifth Avenue in Manhattan one day and stopped for a traffic light next to a well-dressed, middle-aged woman. As we stood there, a strange-looking man, smoking a curved pipe and wearing a golf hat with a big red pompon on top, passed in front of us on an Italian motorcycle. On the seat behind him was a dog, some kind of spaniel, which was wearing the same kind of hat as the master and also had a pipe drooping out its mouth.

I smiled, turned to the lady beside me, and said, "Isn't that crazy!"

She shook her head and replied, "I come out here every day about this time and you really can see some scenes. There are so many unbalanced people in this world."

"You can say that again — well, have a nice day," I said, stepping away from her at the curb.

But she grabbed me by the arm and whispered, "Don't go now!"

"Why not?"

"They're watching from the window, and they'll think we've been together."

I looked toward where she was pointing, saw only open sky, and called out, "We haven't been together!" and directed her to the nearest hospital.

Even after dealing with countless psychotics, I still can't always pick them out right away. This woman was probably suffering from paranoid schizophrenia, a psychosis that made her believe there was some sort of far-reaching conspiracy to pursue and perhaps harm her. After you listen closely to a psychotic for a few minutes, you usually begin to realize that what he's saying doesn't make sense or is far removed from reality.

Psychosis may be caused by an exceptionally serious reaction to some childhood trauma or a chemical imbalance in the brain, which may be inherited. Some insane people are quite easy to recognize. If a person tells you he's God or Jesus Christ or Napoleon, that's fairly obvious. But many times you have to observe a person quite closely if he's a borderline psychotic who hasn't gone completely over the edge. Generally speaking, if your acquaintance has very serious problems adjusting or functioning in ordinary life situations, he may be a borderline case. For example, when a person can't go to work because he can't pull himself out of bed, that's a sure sign something is wrong. People who sleep fourteen hours a day somehow feel they can't cope with life. They can't face the stresses and strains of day-to-day living and are probably suffering from a serious mental disorder. Here are some other characteristics that may accompany psychosis:

1. Inappropriate behavior, such as laughing or crying at strange times.
2. Extreme depression.

3. Hand wringing.
4. Unusual hatred of minority groups: "I'm going to kill me a nigger or a Jew!"
5. Complete disregard for personal hygiene or normal standards of social conduct.
6. Frank threats to commit suicide.

Suicide bears further discussion because this is an increasing phenomenon which you may well encounter at some point. First of all, if anyone threatens to commit suicide in your presence, do everything in your power to get the person to a professional therapist immediately. Suicidal personalities are insidiously expert in drawing well-meaning lay counselors into their web of influence so that escape without emotional scars may be impossible.

One clergyman called me up and said he had gotten into trouble counseling a woman who had been threatening suicide. "She's been coming in to see me every day, and all my other appointments have been fouled up," he said. "But I don't see how I can just tell her to leave me alone, because she might actually do it — go out and kill herself."

"Have you told her she's getting in the way of other people who need your help?" I asked.

"Yes, but she just says, 'I'll hurt myself and you'll be sorry.' "

"She's expressing her hostility to you and people in general by draining you of your time and energy. She's also focused on you as the only way she can be healed — she's put a mantle of omnipotence on you, and you've made the mistake of accepting it."

"So what can I do?" he asked.

"Send her over to me."

But when the minister told this woman, whose name was Rachel, that she'd have to see me from then on, she refused. He called me back and said, "She won't go along with it."

"*Make* her go along with it!" I said. "Tell her you won't see her any more."

"I'm frightened. She might kill herself."

I sighed, "It must be wonderful to be omnipotent," I said. "I'm glad I don't have that responsibility and can leave some things up to God.''

He laughed and sent Rachel over. The first thing she said when she sat down in a chair in my office was, ''I'm going to kill myself.''

''Rachel, you're old enough to make that decision,'' I replied calmly. ''If you're really intent on killing yourself, there's nothing your priest or I can do. But I think you're manipulating us, and you're actually hurting yourself more than anyone else. The pastor told me you haven't had a job in more than a year — now why don't you go to work? I think that would be a good first step . . .''

But before I could finish she began to rant and rave until my office echoed with profanity. She finally left the room, went back to her priest, and said, ''Why did you send me to that quack?''

Hard as it was for him, he refused to counsel her and told her to go back to me. Instead of returning immediately, she got a job and finally made an appointment with me a few weeks later. I learned then that her mother had never shown her love and she felt she had to manipulate people to get love out of them. Suicide threats had served this purpose on a number of occasions.

Suicide threats always have to be taken very seriously, but you should never plead with a person not to kill himself. If you do plead, then he'll continue to use the threats in the effort to get you to show concern and compassion. The best approach to a suicidal person is to listen to his problem with feeling, assure him that help is available, and then send for that help — a professional therapist of some sort. You should schedule an interview with the professional while the person is sitting with you. If the threats seem quite immediate — "I'm going to kill myself when I walk outside your office" — call the police or the person's relative. That will usually take the wind out of his sails or at least put the burden of deterrence in the hands of people who have more power than you to exercise control.

A priest I know has one of the most effective and balanced responses I've ever heard in dealing with the occasional suicidal people who come to him for help. In a warm tone of voice, he says, "I'm not competent to handle this situation, and I want to set up an appointment for you with a professional therapist. I really want to help you, and this is the best way I know how to do it. If you won't go see this person, then there's nothing I can do. You know as well as I do that if you're intent on killing yourself, you'll accomplish it. I don't want to see you do it because I know that's not what God's plan is for you. You have too much potential to throw your life away. But there's nothing I can do if you've made up your mind."

When you've reached the point in counseling where you know you can't do the person any more good, the best thing you can do is call in someone with more training and experience. Effective counseling may take weeks, months, or even years and if you don't see any healing taking place, the best thing to do is to step out of the picture and let someone else try to help. The problem you're trying to correct may not be the real problem at all, and the longer the person waits to have his emotional wounds healed, the more likely it is that he may face permanent or even fatal psychological damage.

Chapter Sixteen

The Freedom of the Spirit

My main objective in these pages has not been to transform you into an amateur psychoanalyst, but rather to acquaint you with some of the practical principles of therapy that can facilitate love and emotional healing. Jesus said, "Love your enemies and pray for those who persecute you". (Matthew 5:44). If you *understand* why a person is acting hostilely, it's easier to love him and respond to him constructively. If you don't try to understand, you're likely to react in kind — take an eye for an eye and a tooth for a tooth. In psychological terms, you'll start "countertransferring" your own emotional problems and deficiencies, and the result will be anything but love.

There is a recurrent New Testament theme relating to Christian love therapy which I like to call the *two-person principle*. There are a number of verses which we have traditionally associated with worship services and prayer meetings, but which are equally applicable to one-on-one counseling sessions. Jesus said, for example, "if two of you on earth agree to ask anything at all, it will be granted to you by my Father in heaven. For where two or three meet in my name, I shall be there with them." (Matthew 18:19 - 20). If the two people are a Christian counselor and a person with an emotional problem, the possibilities of this passage for therapy are enormous. If you are honest and open as you counsel with your spouse or friend and if your prayers come from pure motives, God promises healing: "So confess your sins to one another, and pray for one another, and this will cure you. The heartfelt prayer of a good man works very powerfully." (James 5:16).

As two people meet together for a discussion of an emotional difficulty, the person who assumes the Good Parent role must above all other things be supportive, patient, and compassionate. One of the most meaningful scriptural guidelines I've encountered to back this approach comes from the letter to the Hebrews: " . . . let us be concerned for each other, *to stir a response in love and good works*. Do not stay away from the meetings of the community, as some do, the more so as you see the Day drawing near." (Hebrews 10:24 - 25 [emphasis added]). Whenever I've assumed this attitude of spiritual support in dealing with those who come to me for help, healing has always occurred. The repressed bitterness, hate, and hostility that often boil up into emotional disturbances cannot retain their demonic power in a confrontation with Christian love.

The individuals with whom you work in these two-person encounters must be treated not as cases, but as unique human beings in need of love. But it's still important to provide God's Spirit with a systematic framework for expressing that love. You'll probably find the greatest power in healing if you focus on these three keys to spiritual freedom in Christian love therapy:

1. Outline your friend's problem in detail. If you can remember every relevant thing he tells you about himself, then you may not need to use pen and paper. But until you gain some experience in dealing with emotional problems, I recommend that most of you write down the important features of your friend's background, personality, and attitudes toward himself. Sometimes it's also helpful to get him to write down what he thinks his problem is and how he can solve it. Putting down these points on paper can help a person objectify and analyze his own emotional wounds and it provides a factual foundation to facilitate the healing process.

2. Be open and vulnerable in your conversations. If your friend gets the impression you're acting like some haughty, self-sufficient sage — or you seem to be just a nosy busybody — he's likely to have trouble relating to you.

There are dark recesses in everybody's personality that are hard to talk about, but often these embarrassing subjects are the most important in understanding an emotional hurt. Your disturbed friend is most likely to talk intimately and honestly if you open the way to deep spiritual sharing by disclosing something about yourself that he can identify with. Indiscriminate disclosures can do more harm than good, but a sensitive use of "confessing your sins" and deficiencies can encourage a "Gee I've had feelings just like that" kind of response. A genuine relationship always involves some sacrifice, including the sacrifice of privacy, if necessary.

3. *Move with God's Spirit*. I've mentioned several times that one of the human problems with classic Freudian psychoanalysis is that there is too much of a tendency to limit therapy to certain rigid, preconceived categories. We put certain labels on emotional disturbances and forget that labels don't always tell everything about the workings of the

infinitely complex human mind.

The Spirit of God, on the other hand, can give us a more complete understanding if we let Him move freely in our personal relationships. I remember a Pennsylvania policeman named Dan who came to see me because he was extremely nervous and had started to drink heavily. His anxiety had a specific cause: He felt guilty about taking petty bribes from local merchants on his beat.

"I sometimes just want to run away from my job," he said. "But I've been a cop for twelve years, and I've got to think about my future and pension."

His mother, a sadistic, selfish woman, made him do favors for her and in return she occasionally showed him some affection. He learned to pacify her by running errands, going to extra Novenas with her, and deferring in general to her every whim. Many of these same characteristics surfaced as we got deeper into our therapeutic relationship. He would bring in coffee and sandwiches for me even when I reminded him it wasn't necessary. I was his new mother, and he seemed to feel he had to placate me, just as he had humored his real parent.

Some of Dan's solicitous acts, though, were not rooted in this need to pacify me. They were actually genuine feelings of love, and I believe God gave me the ability to distinguish between the neurotic and authentic expressions of affection. We actually became good friends as our sessions progressed and he felt free to ask me about my own religious beliefs. The Spirit of God seemed to have given him a genuine interest in spiritual matters, and I decided to share with him some of my personal experiences with God. As a result of this freedom I felt in moving with God's Spirit, Dan renewed his commitment to Christ and became quite active in the Catholic charismatic movement.

Some professional psychoanalysts would say that I went too far, got too personally involved in this relationship. They'd accuse me of using my position to push my religious beliefs, of slipping into subtle forms of countertransference, of acting out my own emotional hang-ups — the list of possible complaints is endless. But the difference between the way I used to operate as a secular analyst and the way I operate now, is that Christ is in ultimate control — not Freud or Adler or some other psychoanalytic guru who has access to only one small part of the truth about personality development.

I related to the policeman Dan, not as a representative of some diagnostic category or even as a patient, but as a man who was hurting terribly as he went through a Calvary of life. By loving him, I showed him how to love. Jesus said, "This is my commandment: love one another, as I have loved you." (John 15:12). He taught his disciples how to love by His own example, and He lives in us and can show our acquaintances the same thing. We can help guide others through their emotional crucifixions by reflecting the love of Christ and the hope of His resurrection in our own lives. If you're really helping a person in a therapeutic love relationship, he'll begin to identify with you. If you have a Western drawl, your friend may start talking with a drawl too. If you walk with a swagger so will he. And if you affirm a Christian value system and a faith in Christ, it's likely that your friend will be drawn through you to God.

So be open to the Lord's guidance in all your personal encounters. Give God's powerful Spirit free rein and relate to others in authentic love. The Apostle Paul has told us, in 1 Corinthians 13, that prophecies will pass away, tongues will cease and knowledge — including popular psychoanalytic knowledge — will fade. The anchor for our lives, the ultimate source of emotional health and meaning, must be firmly embedded in the three qualities which are essential to a relationship with God — faith, hope, and love. "But the greatest of these is love," Paul says. For God Himself is love.